MY CHILDREN'S DAY COLORING BOOK

Large Size 8.5" x 11" inches
(21.59 x 27.94 cm.)

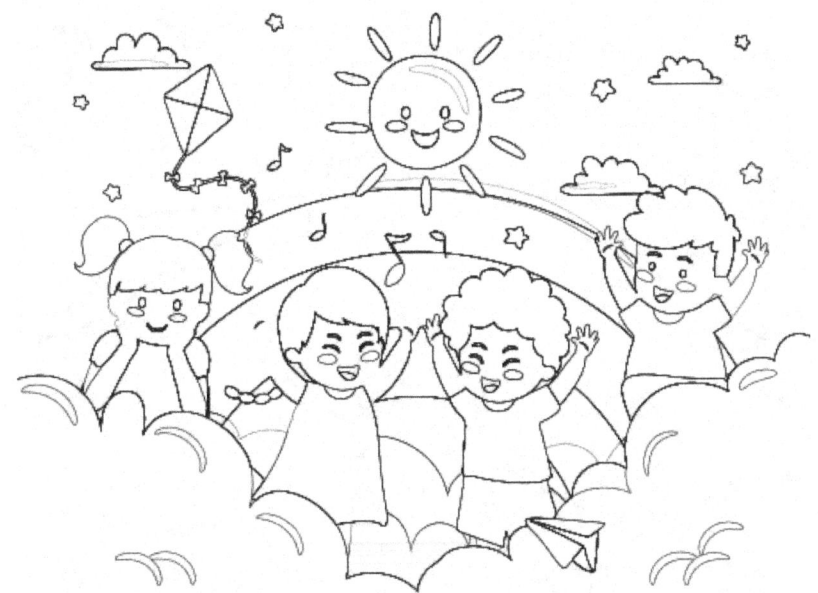

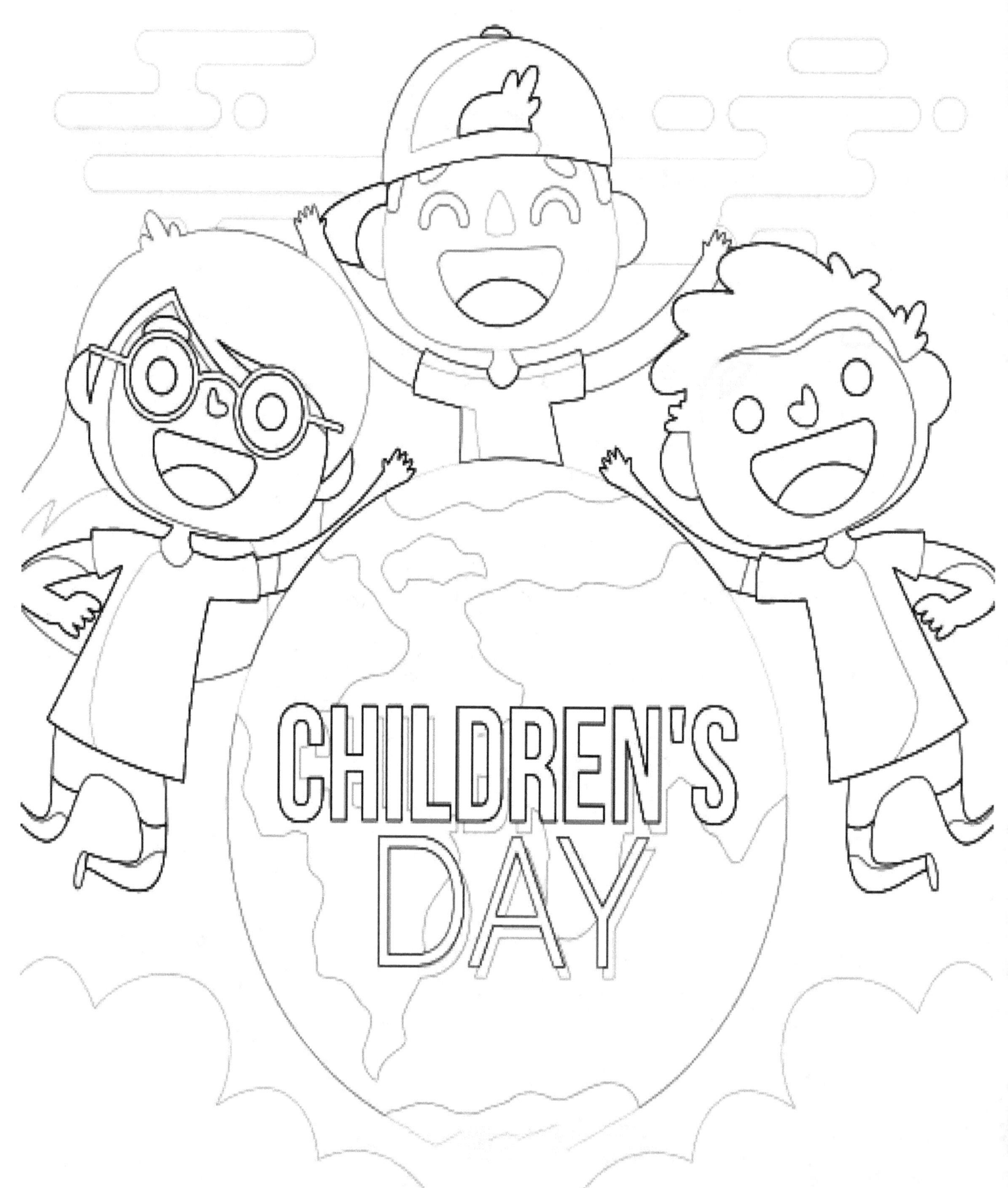

HAPPY CHILDREN'S DAY

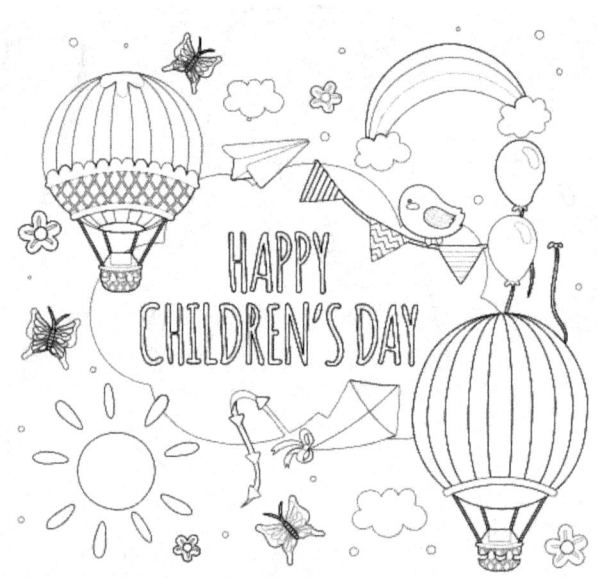

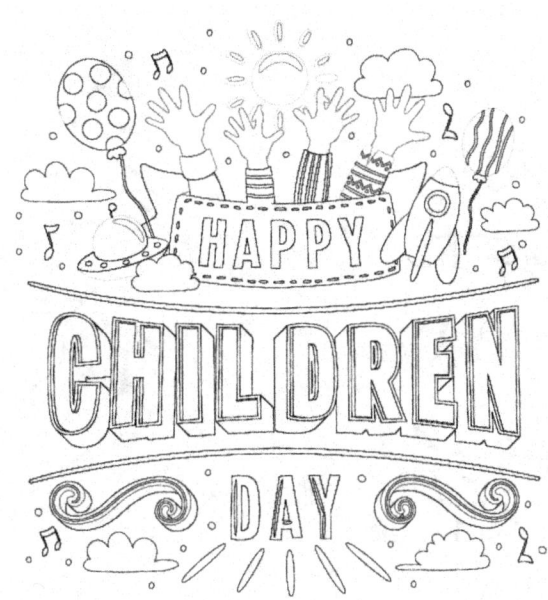

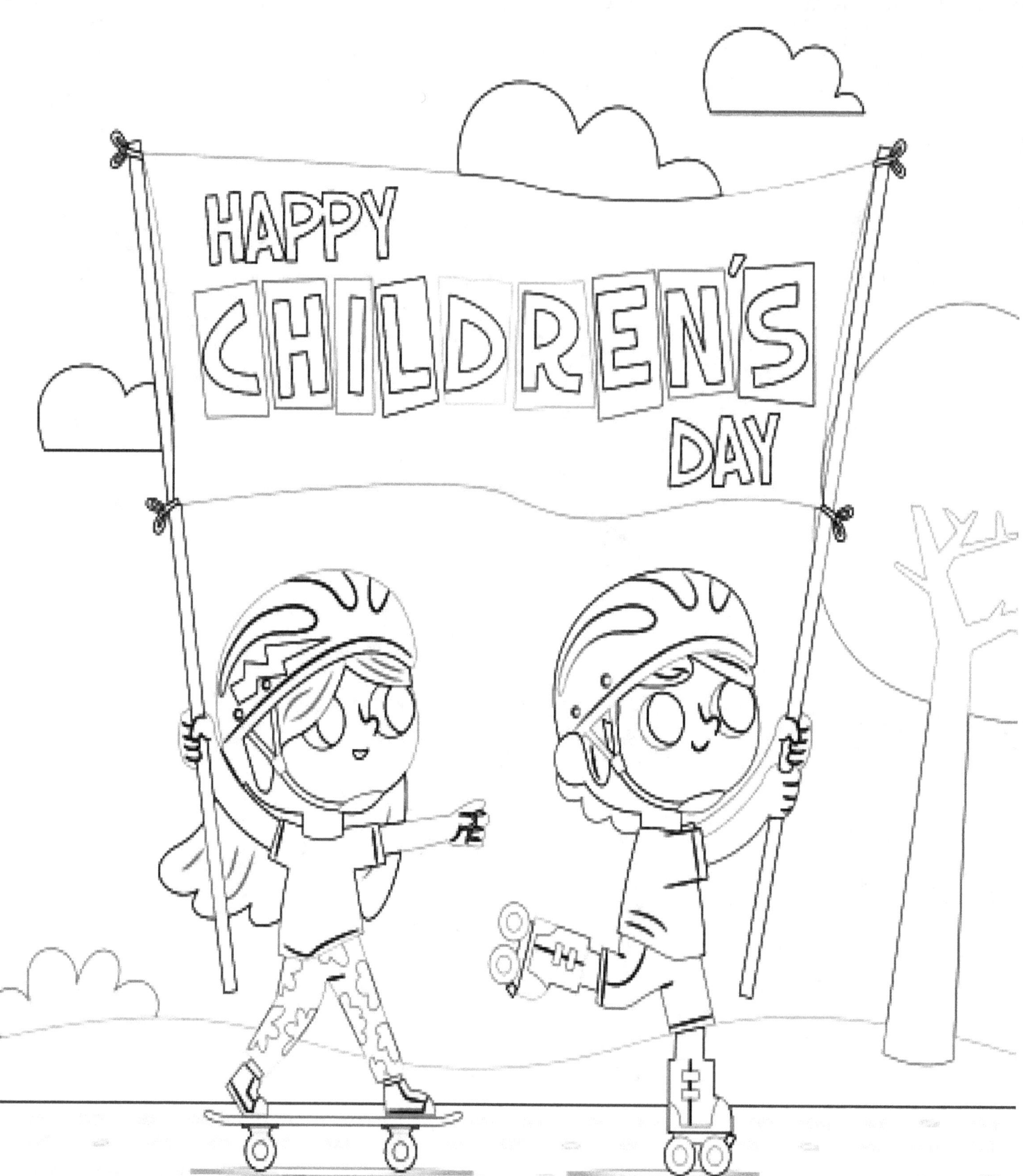

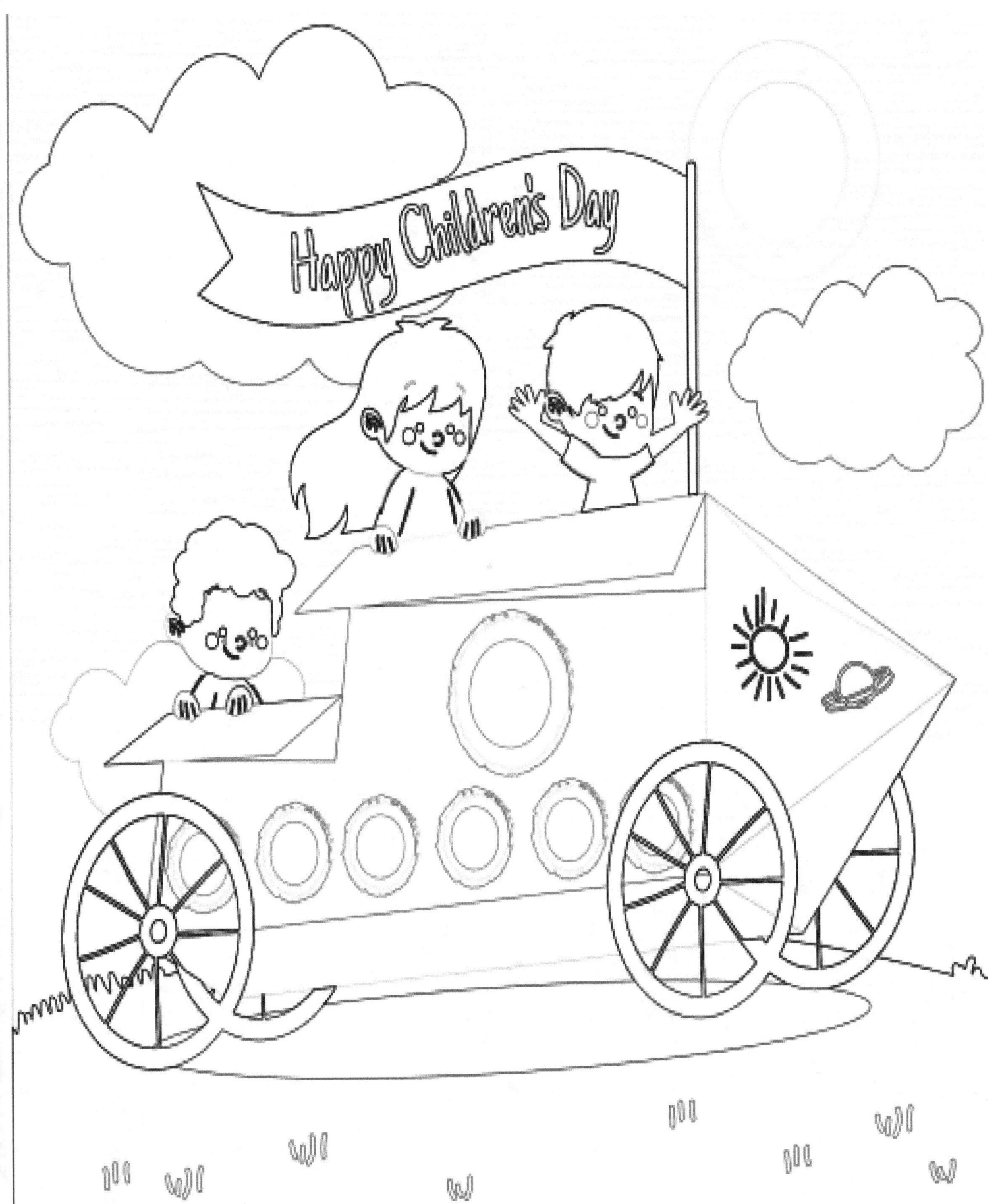

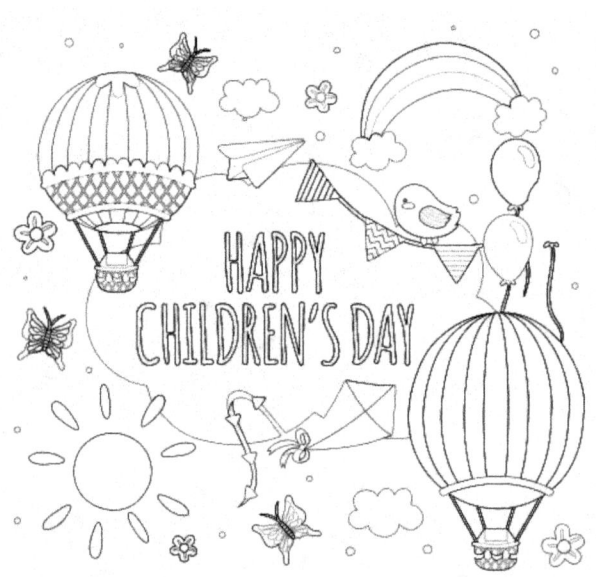

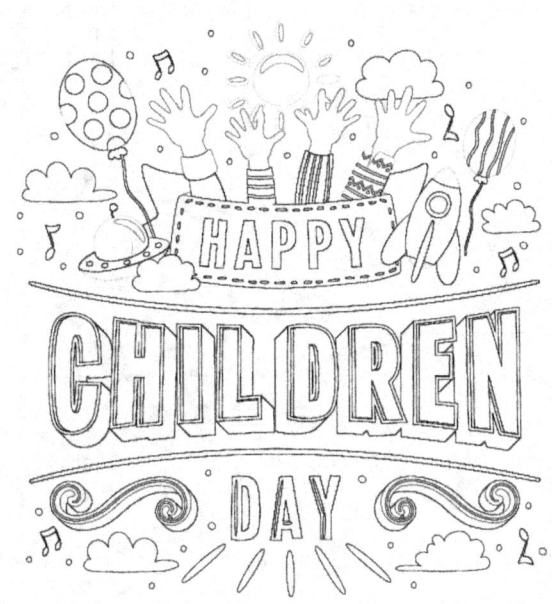

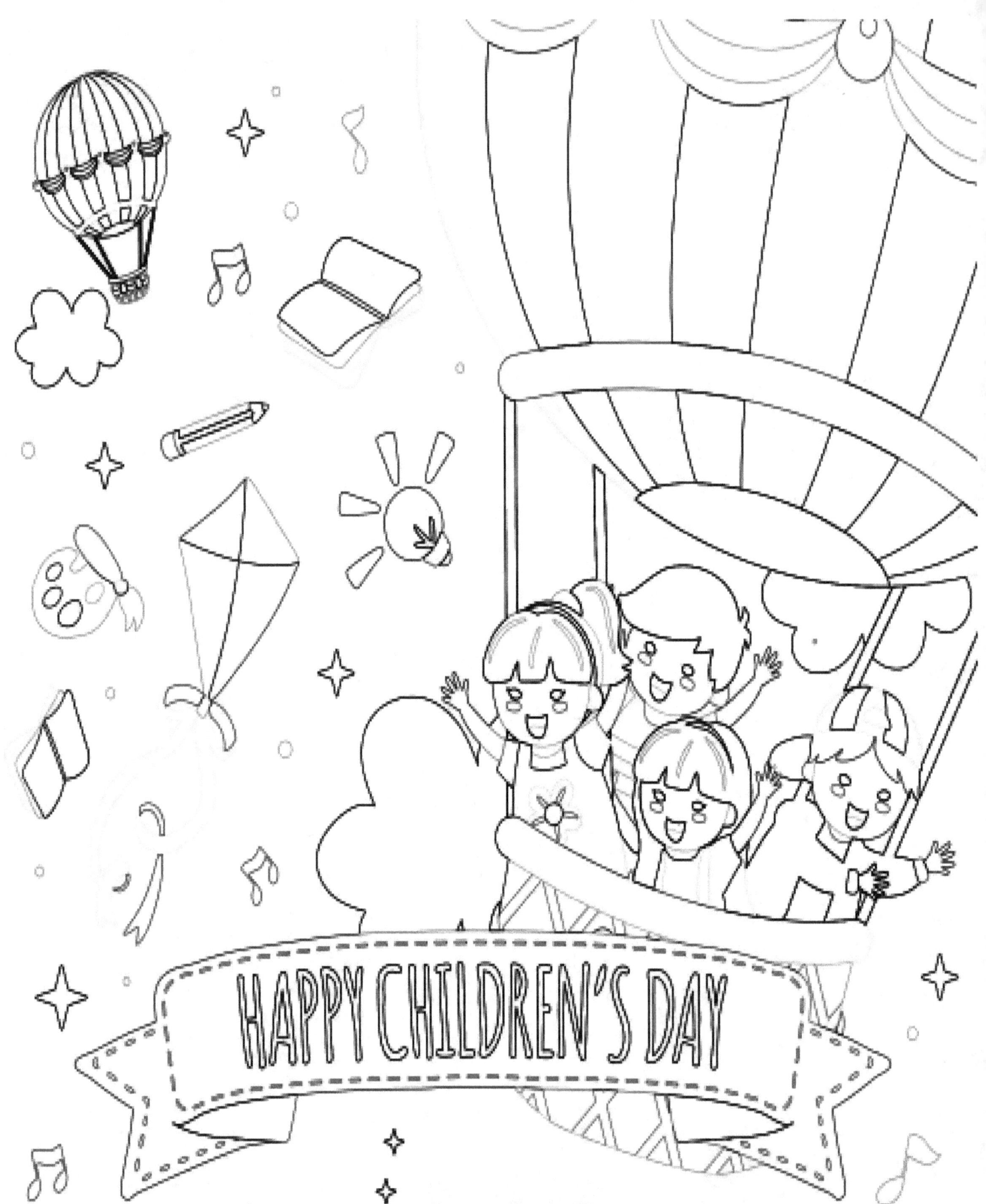

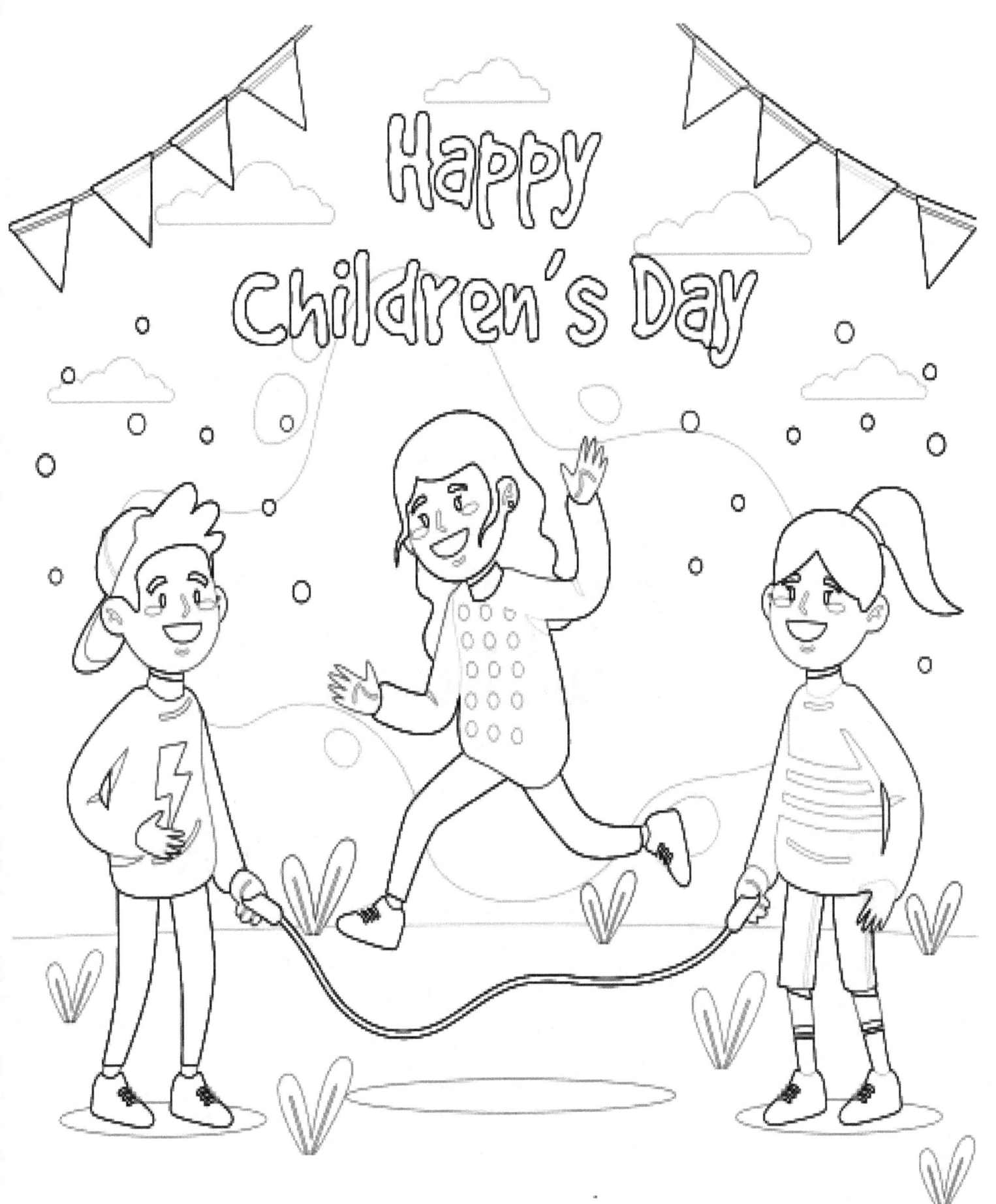

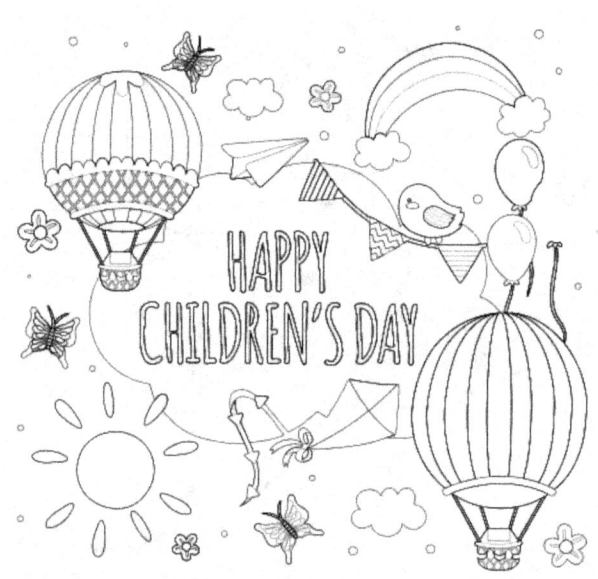

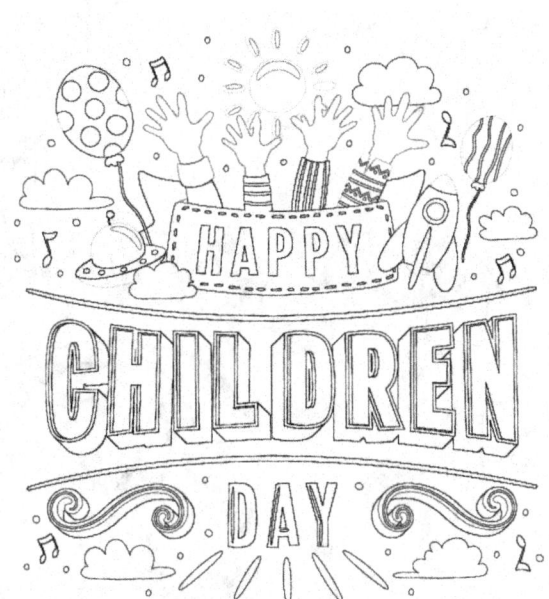

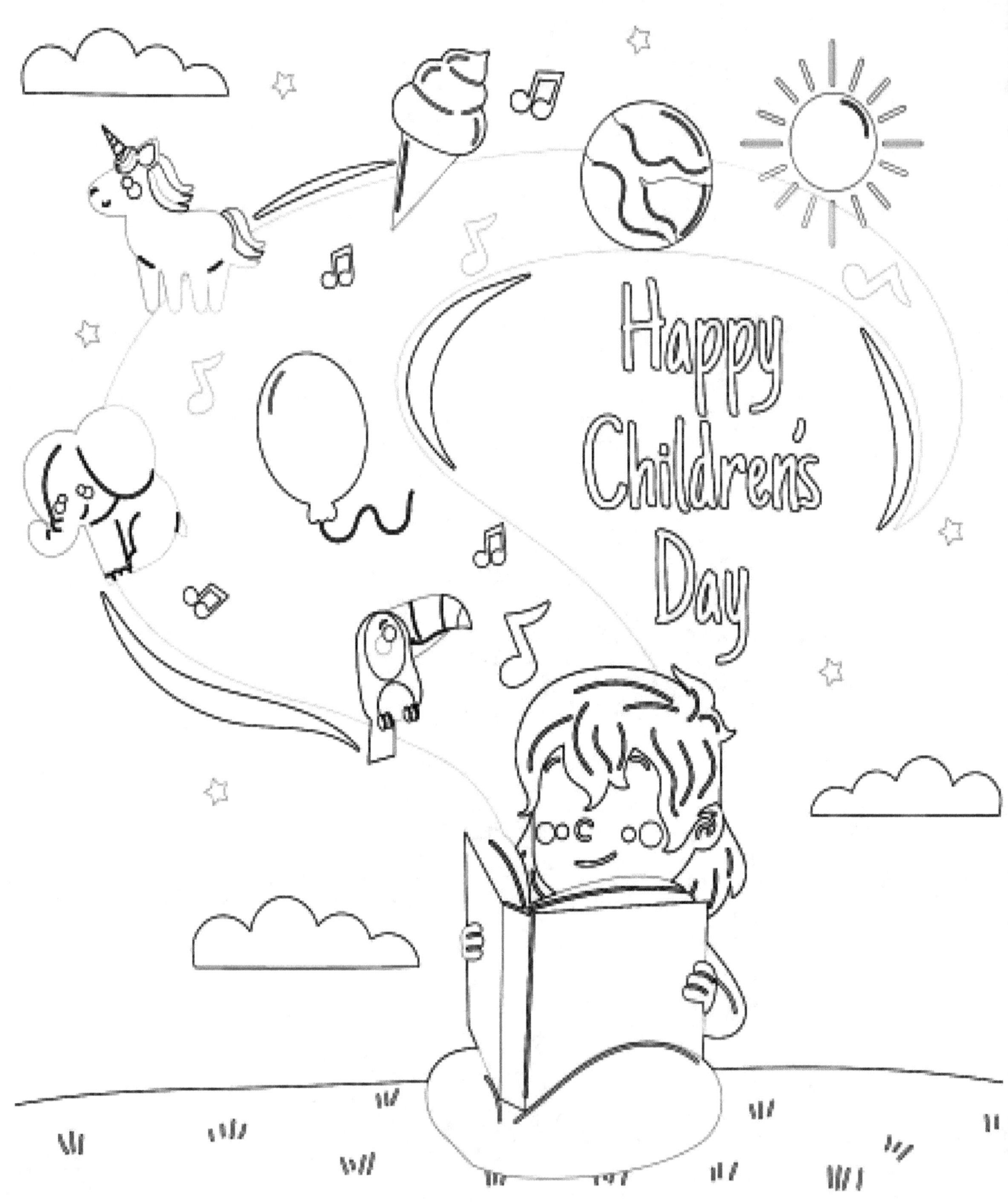

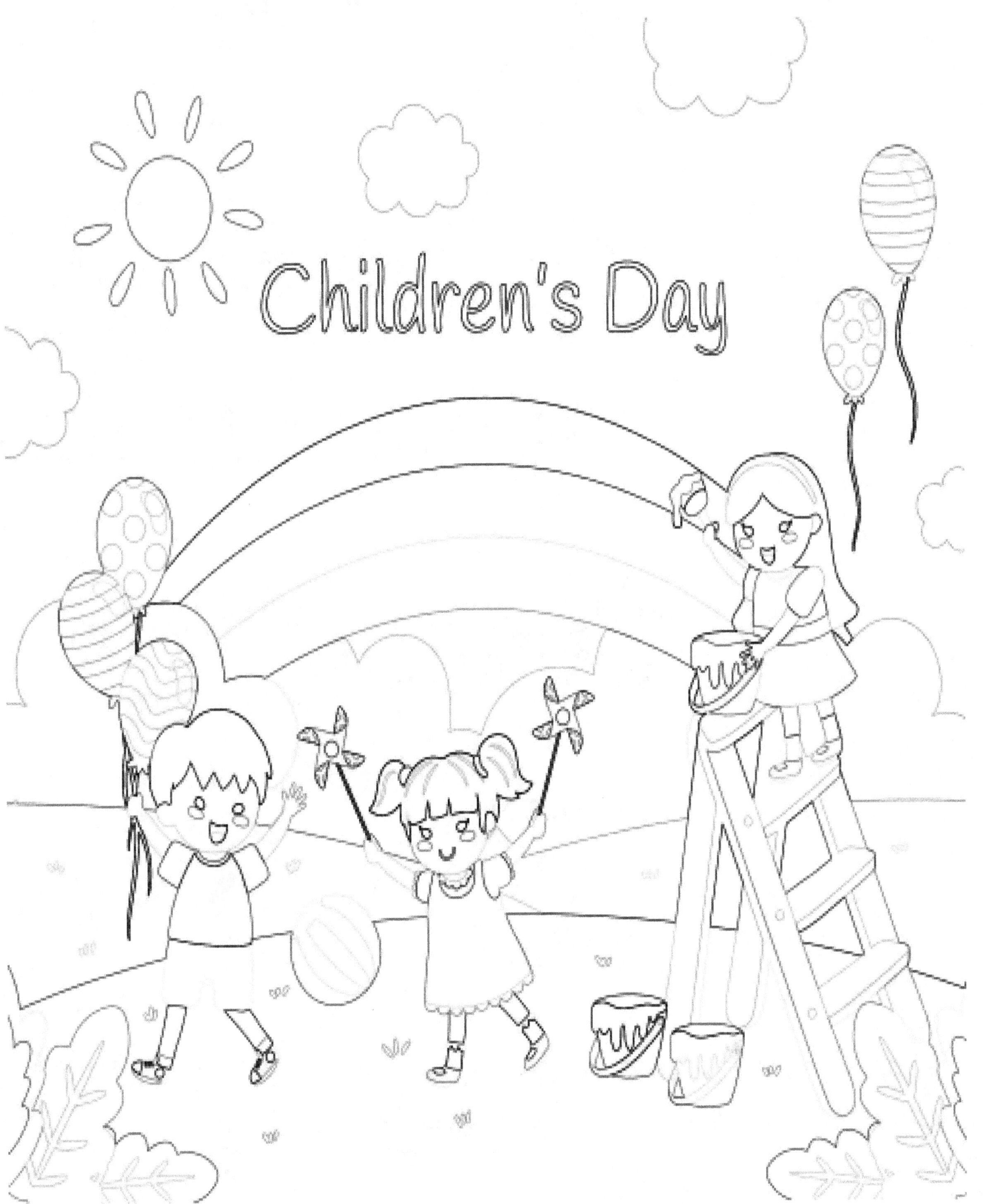

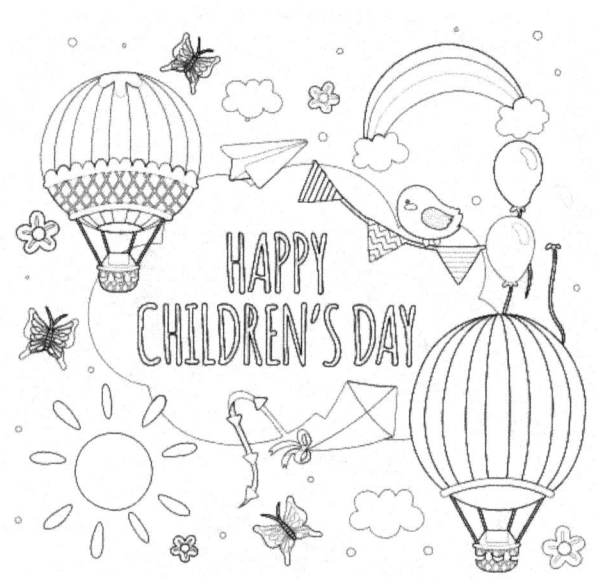

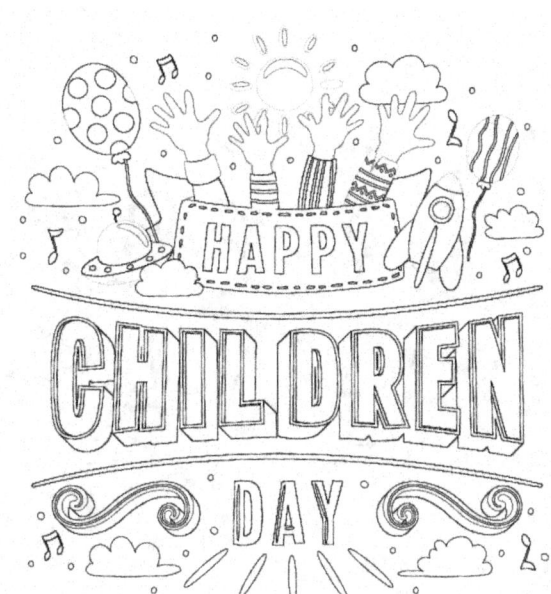

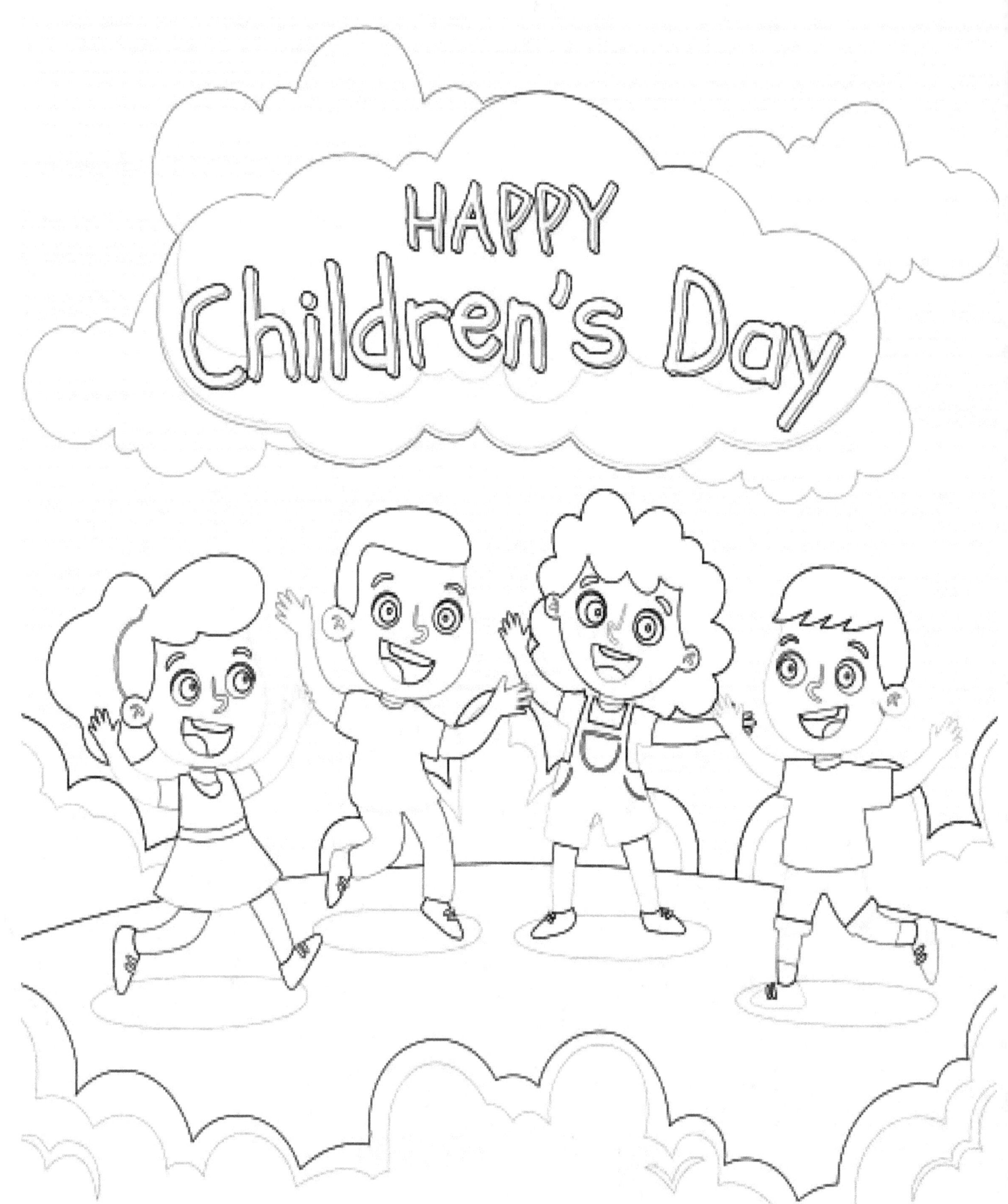

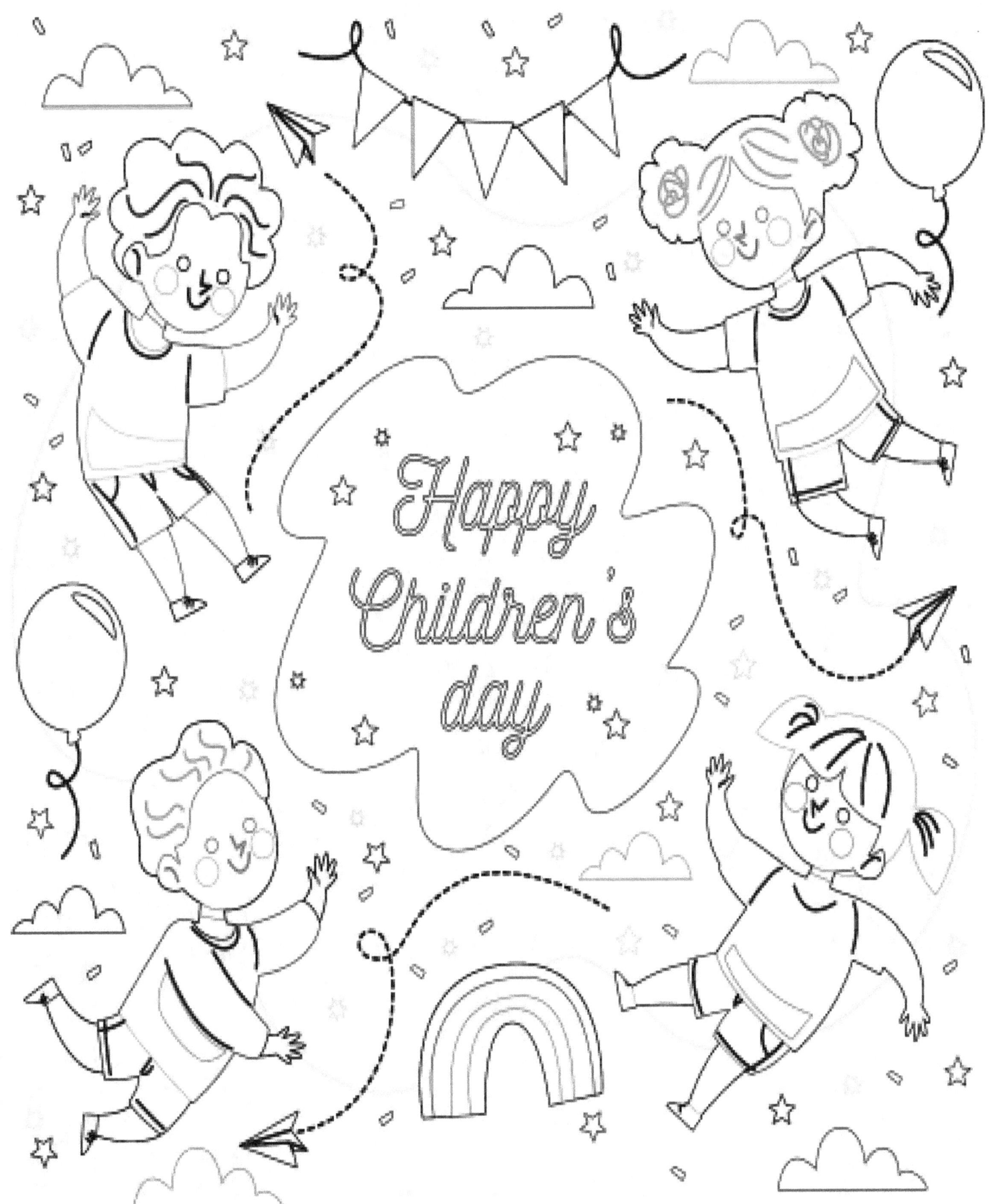

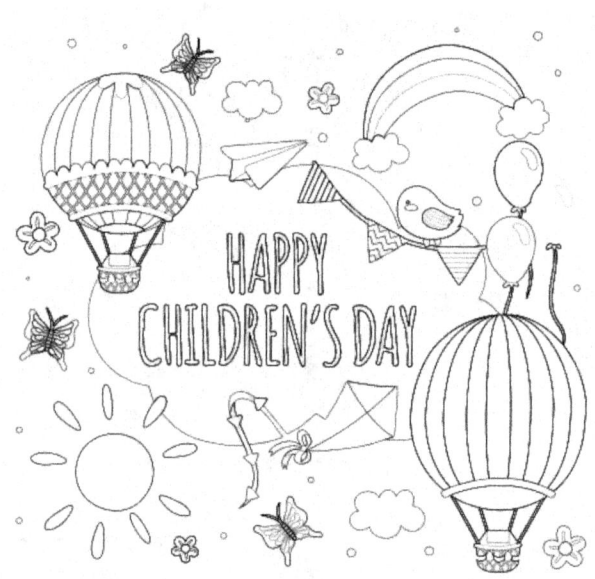

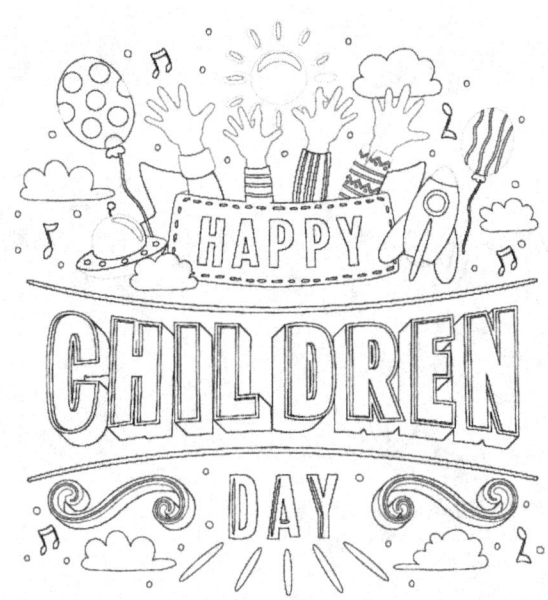

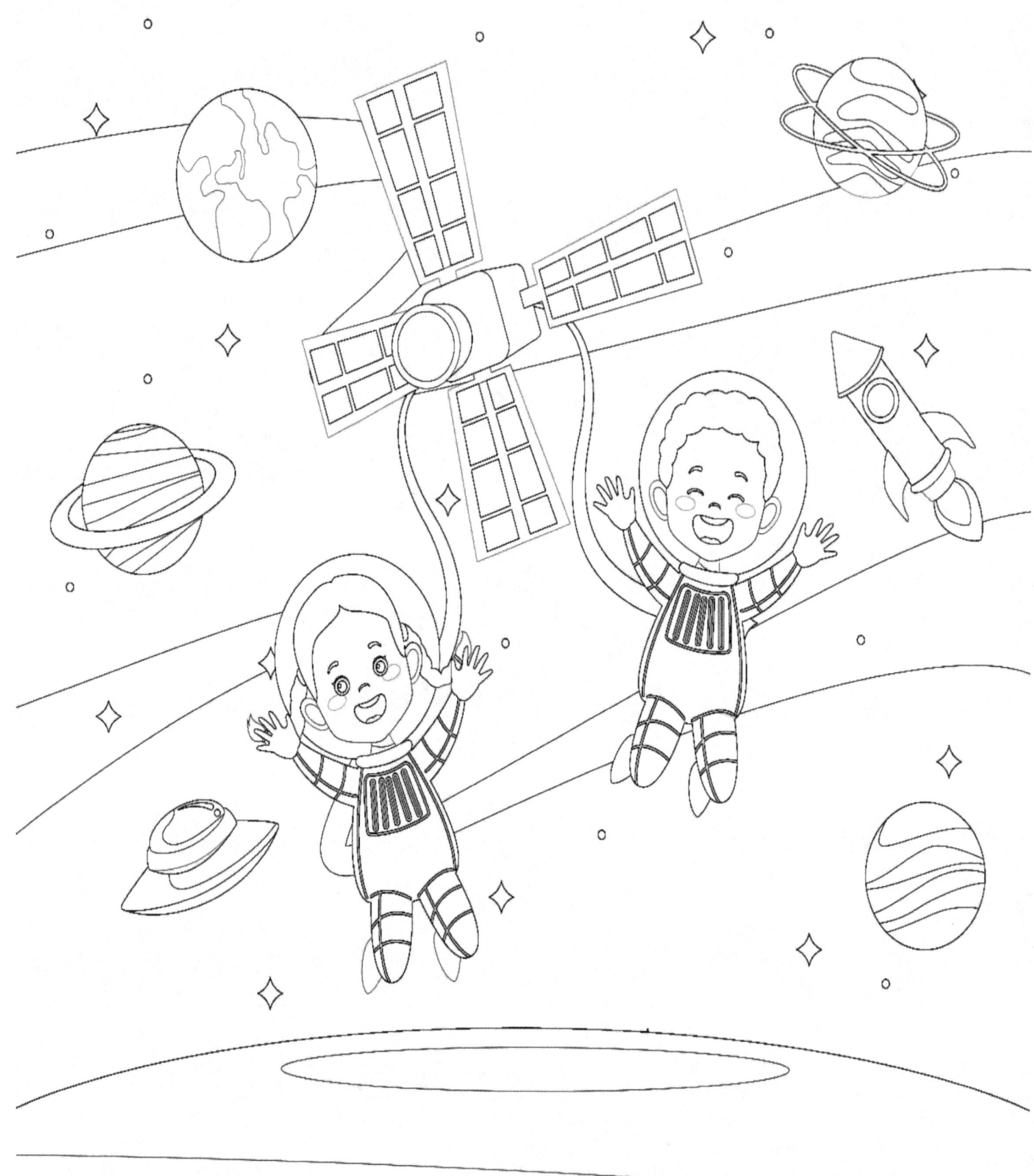

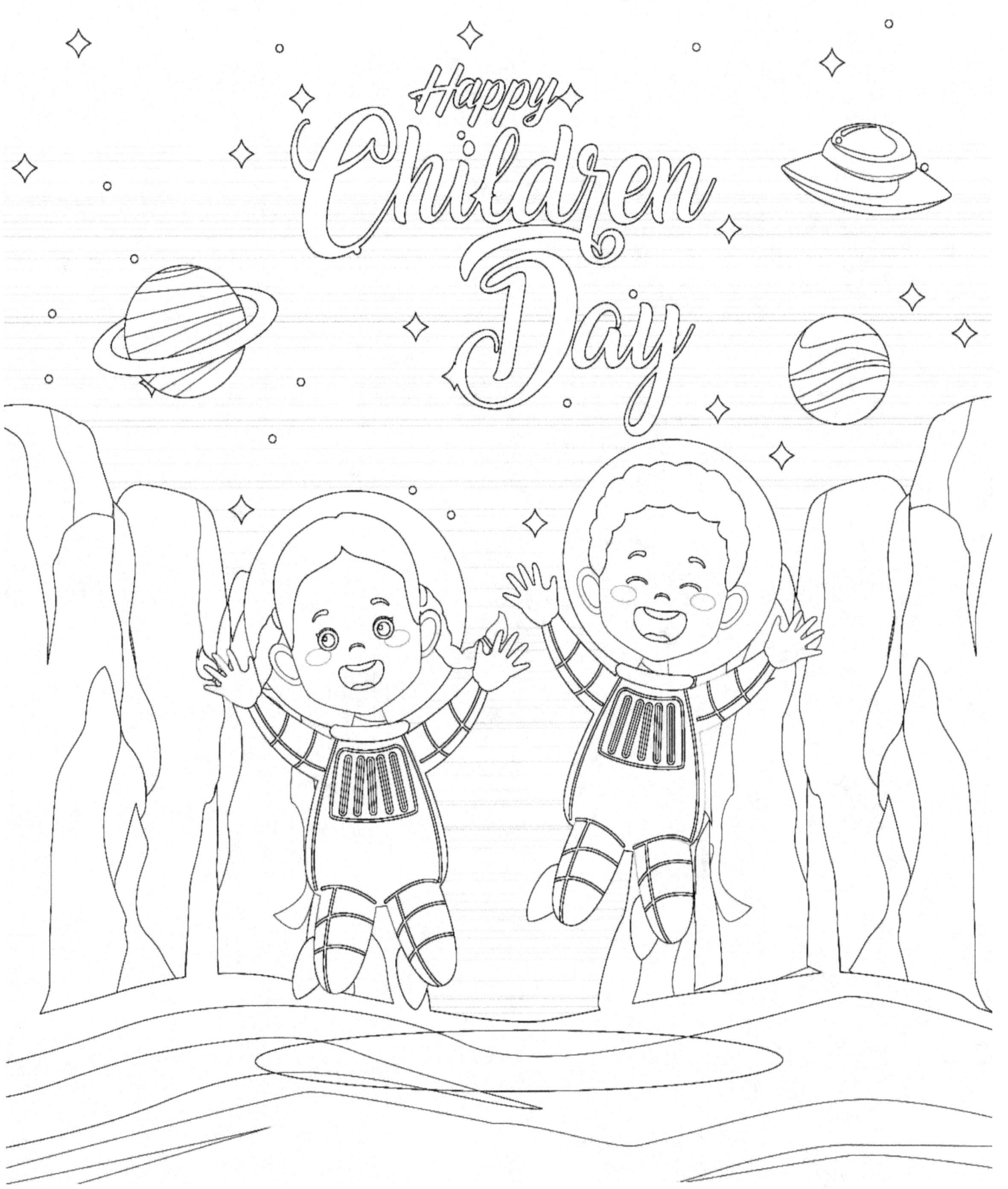

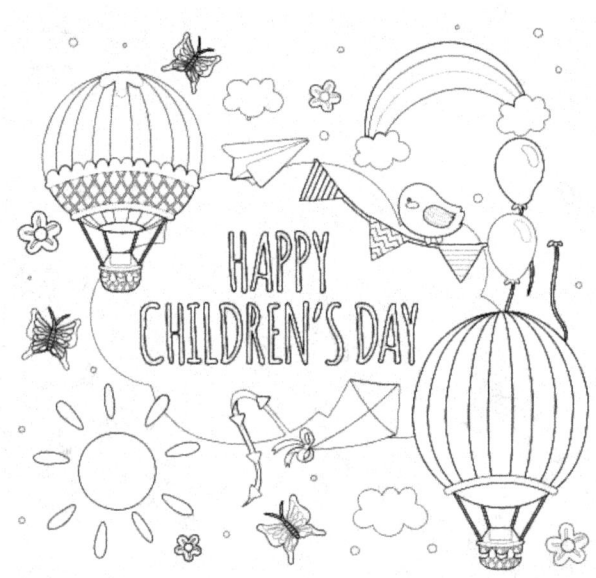

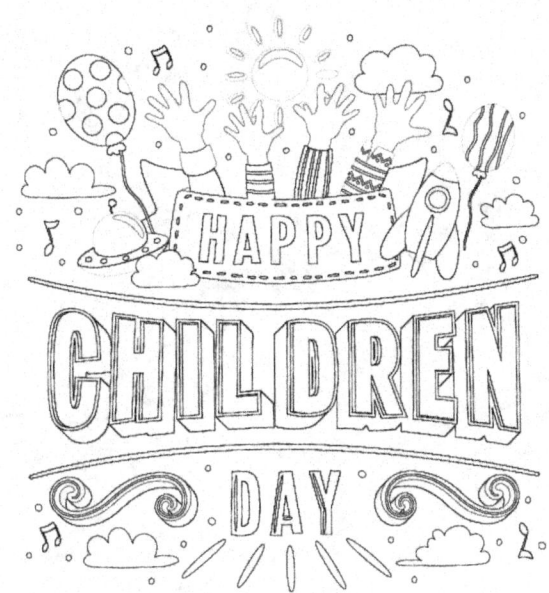

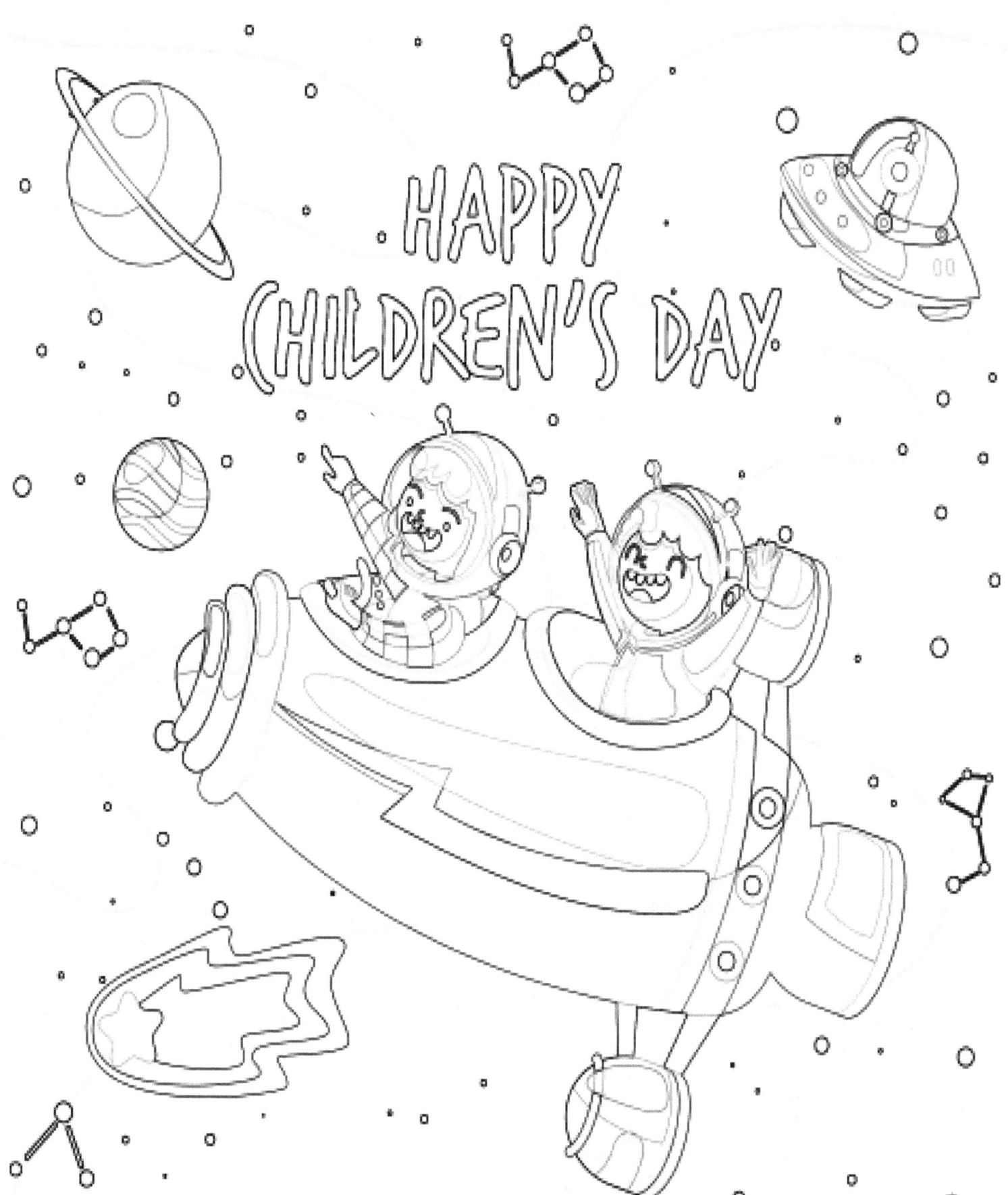

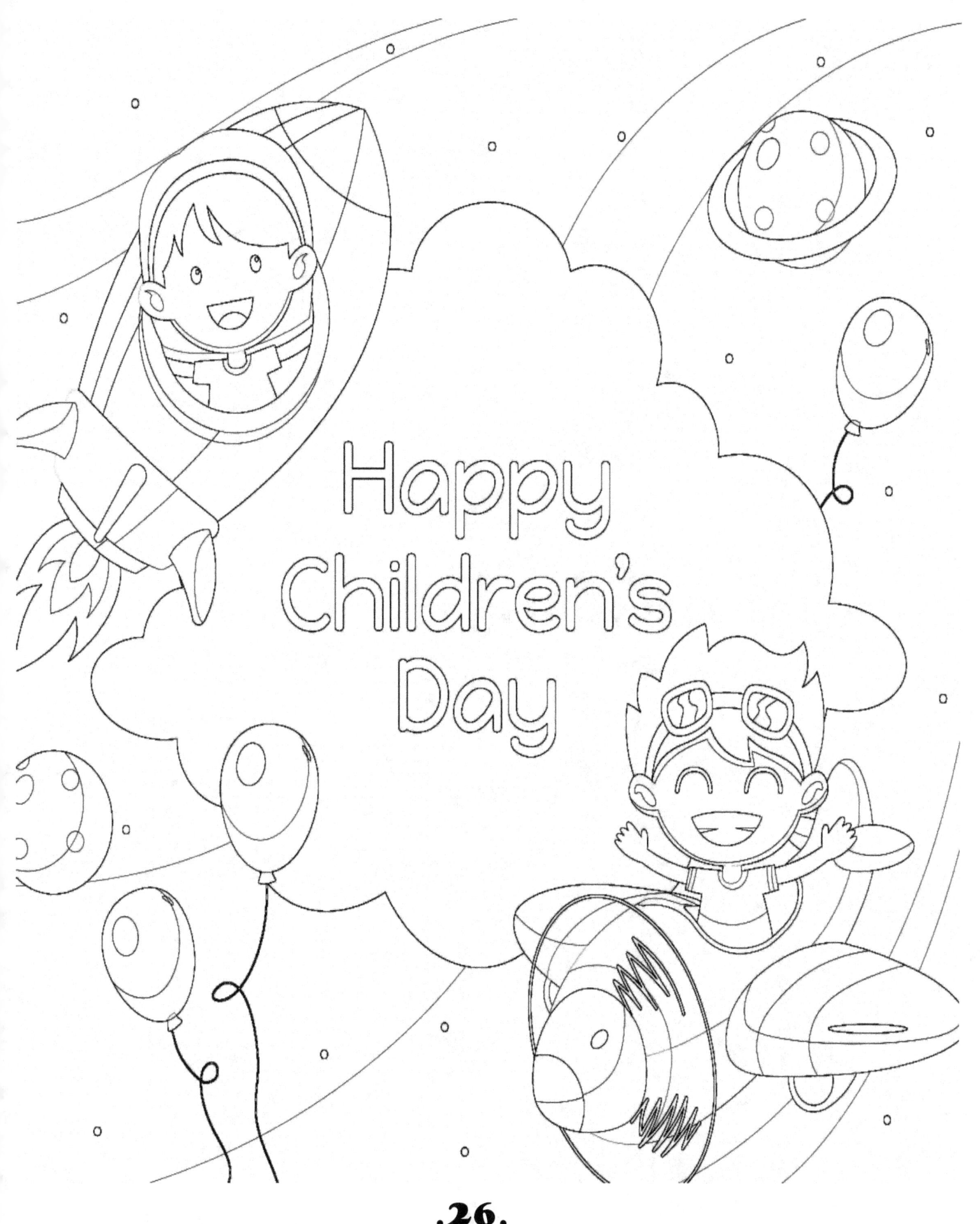

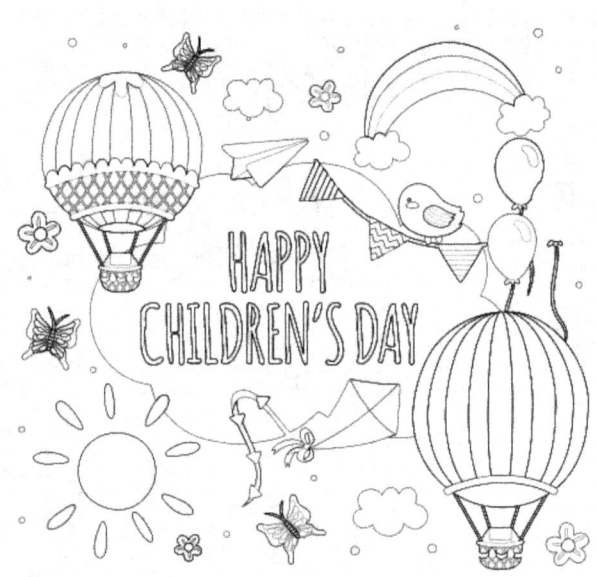

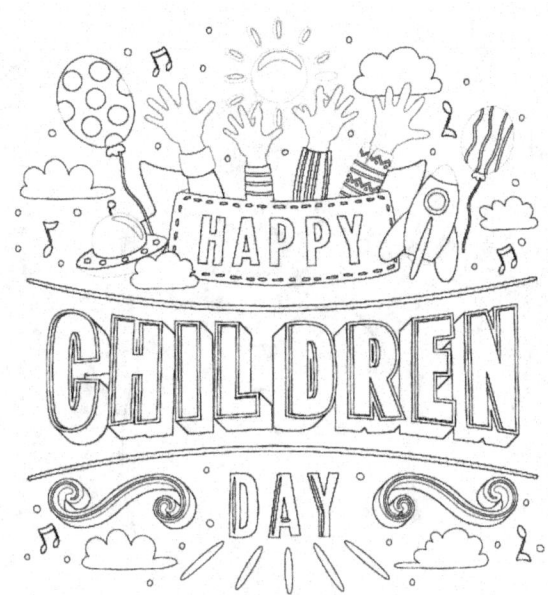

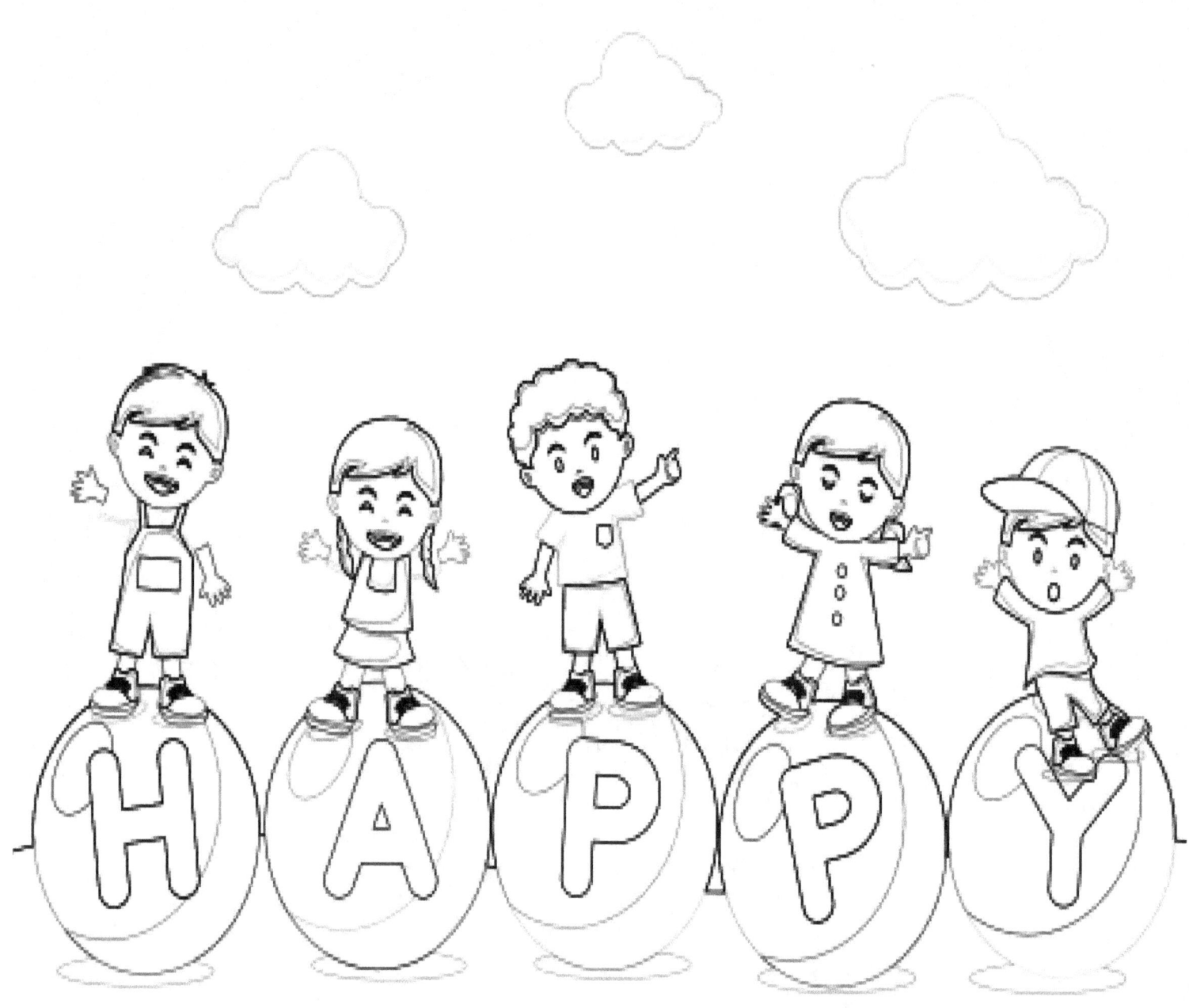

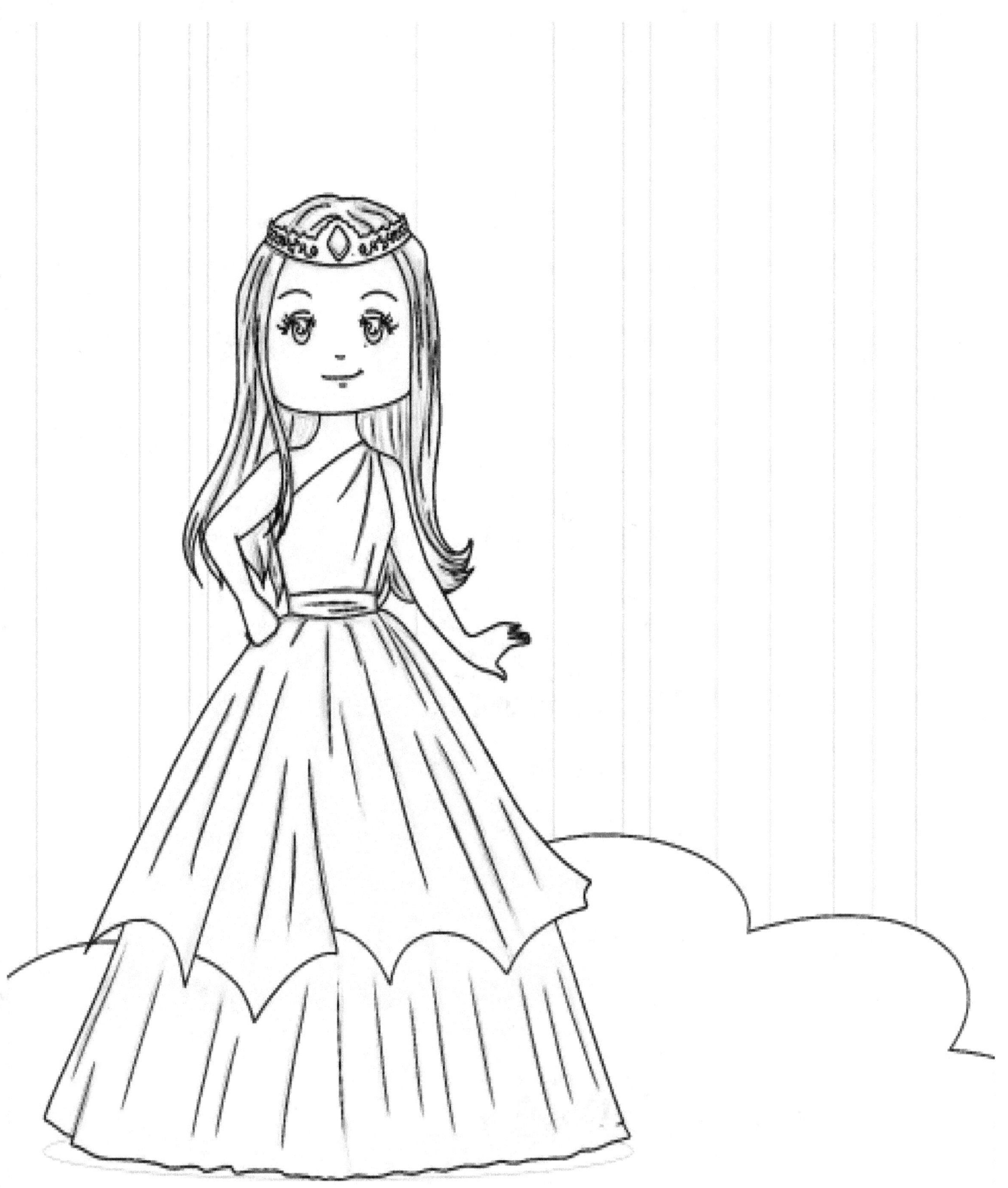

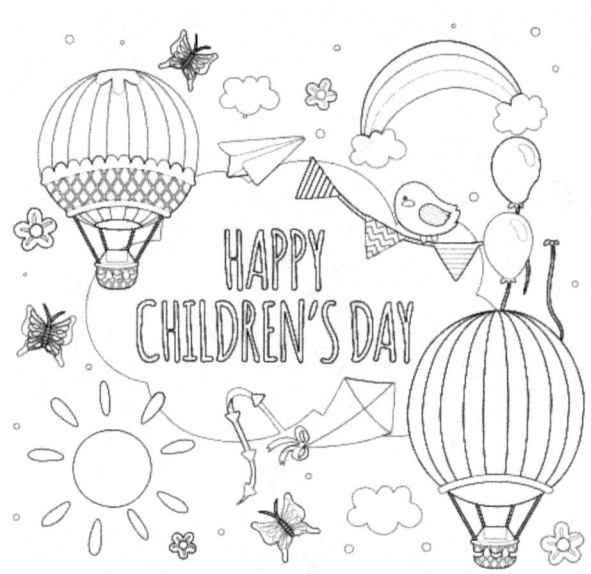

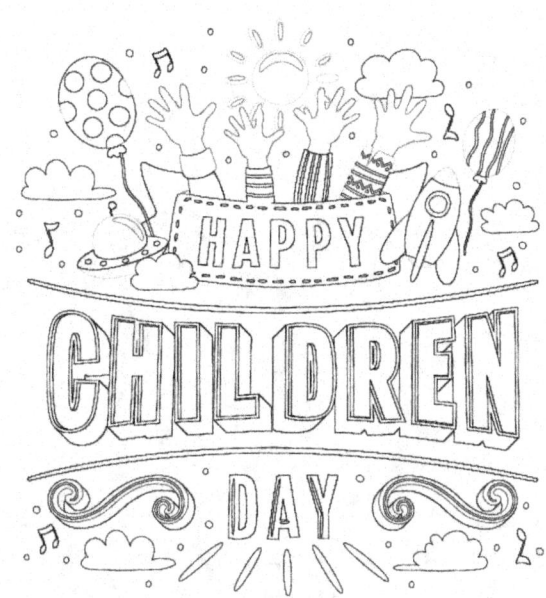

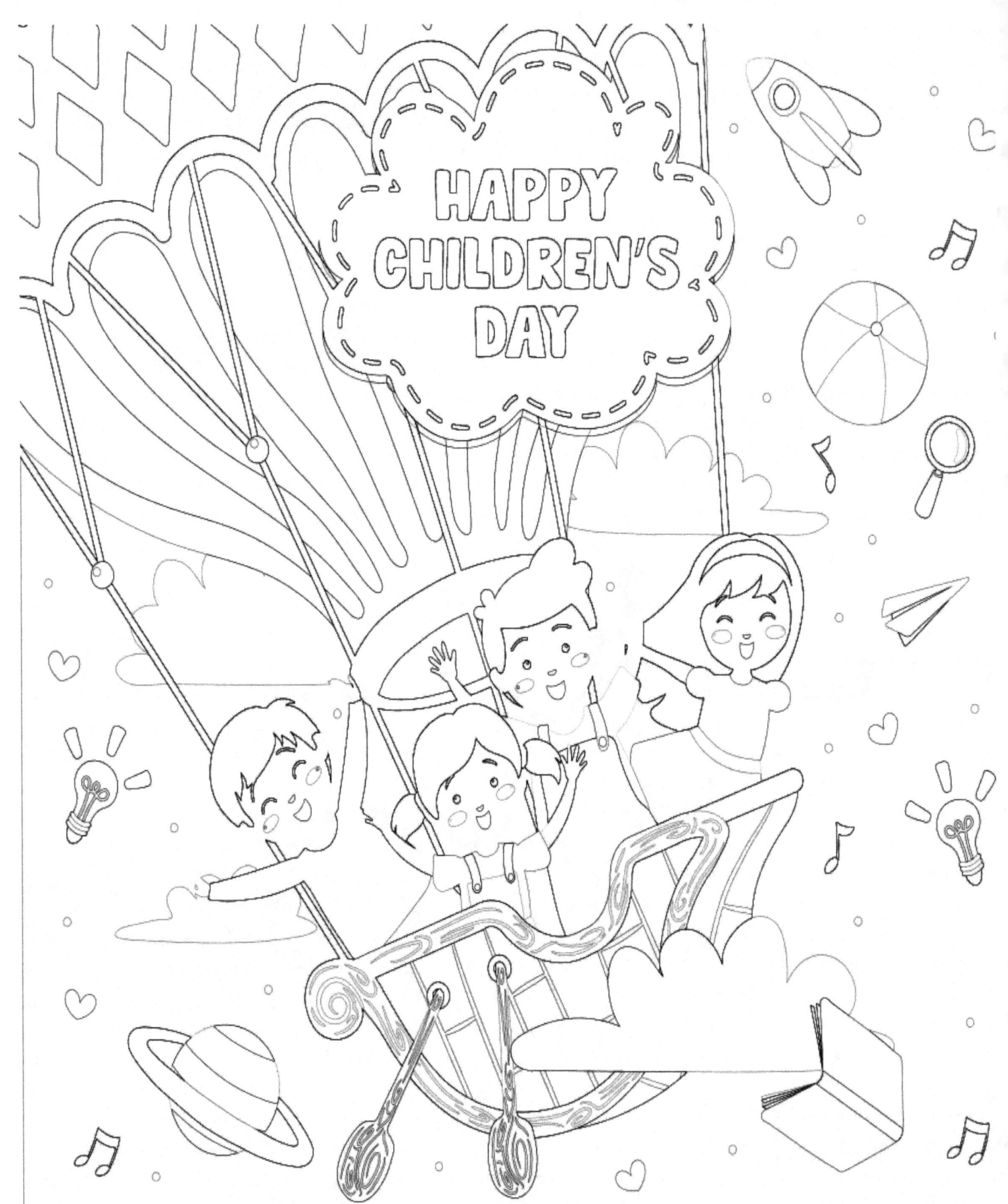

Happy Children's Day

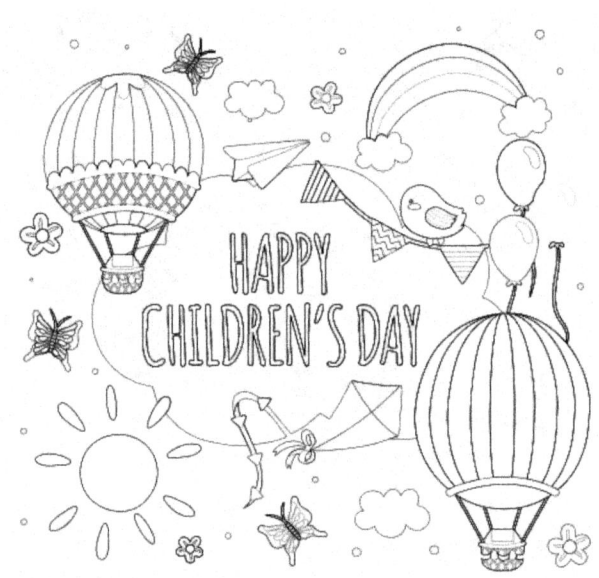

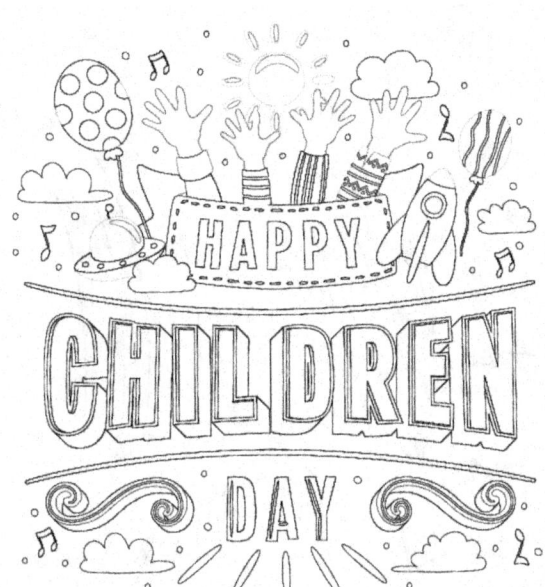

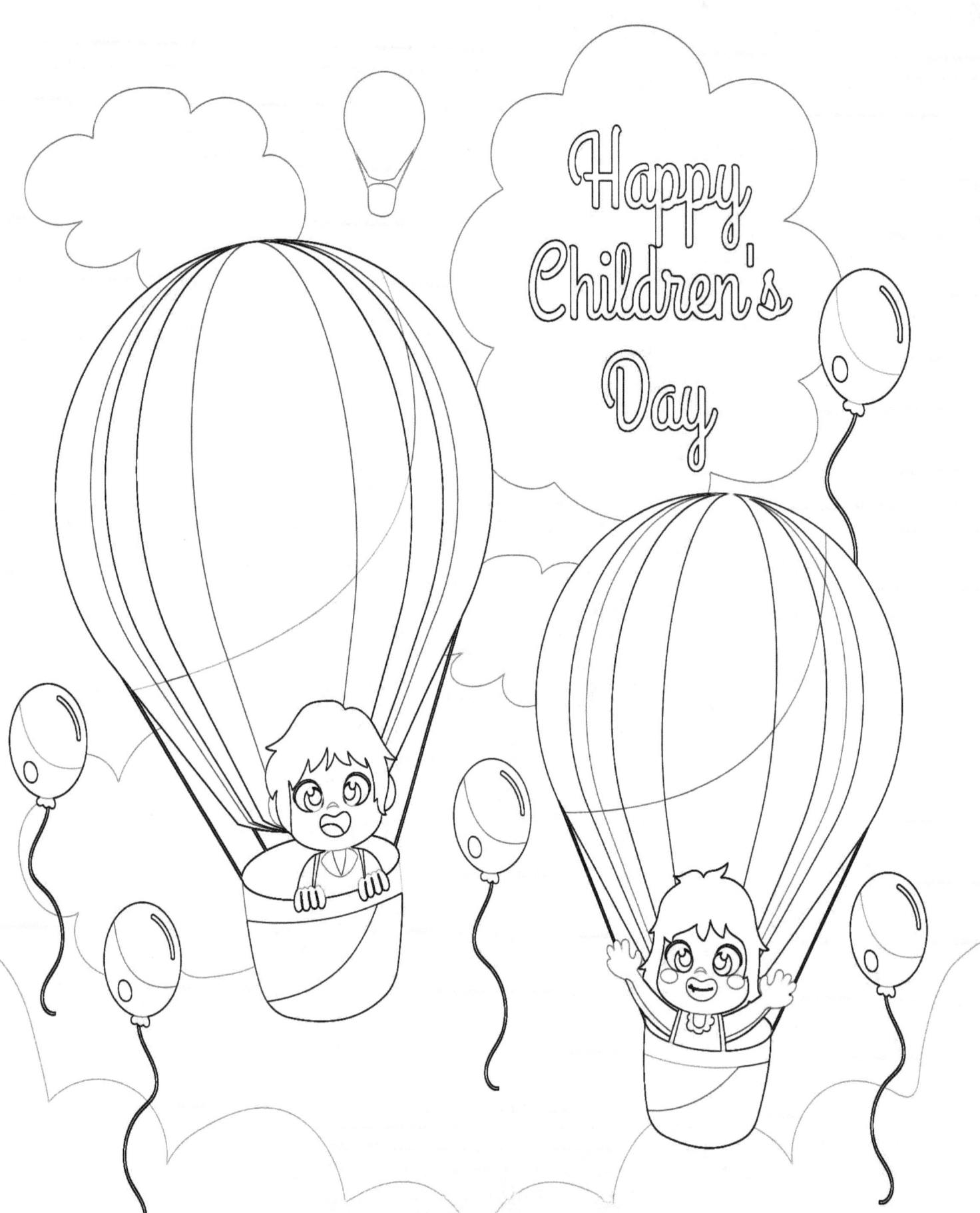

CHILDREN'S DAY

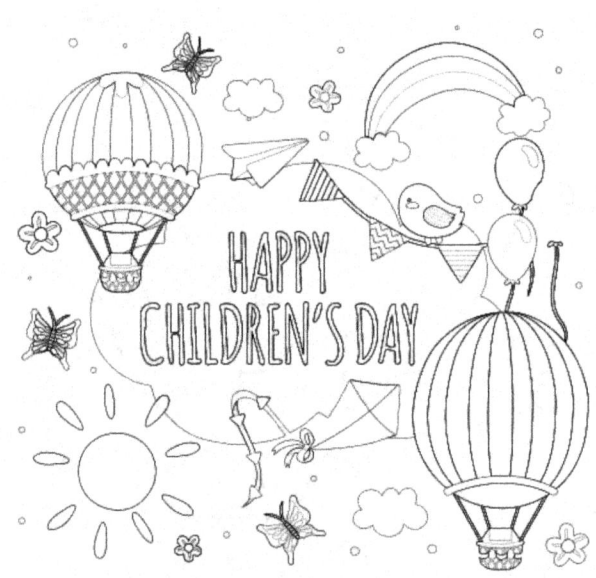

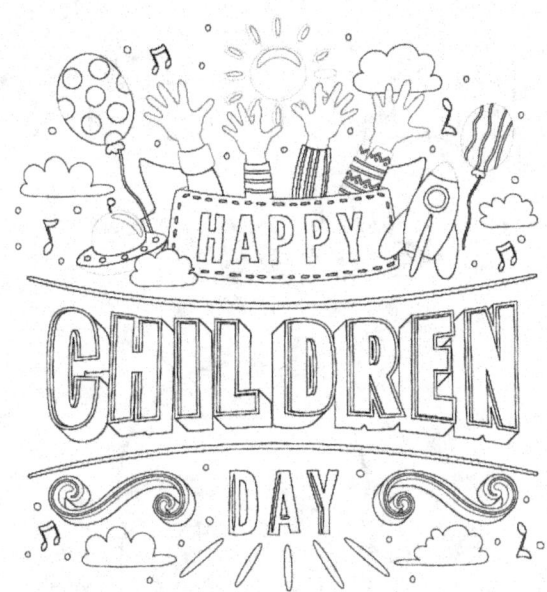

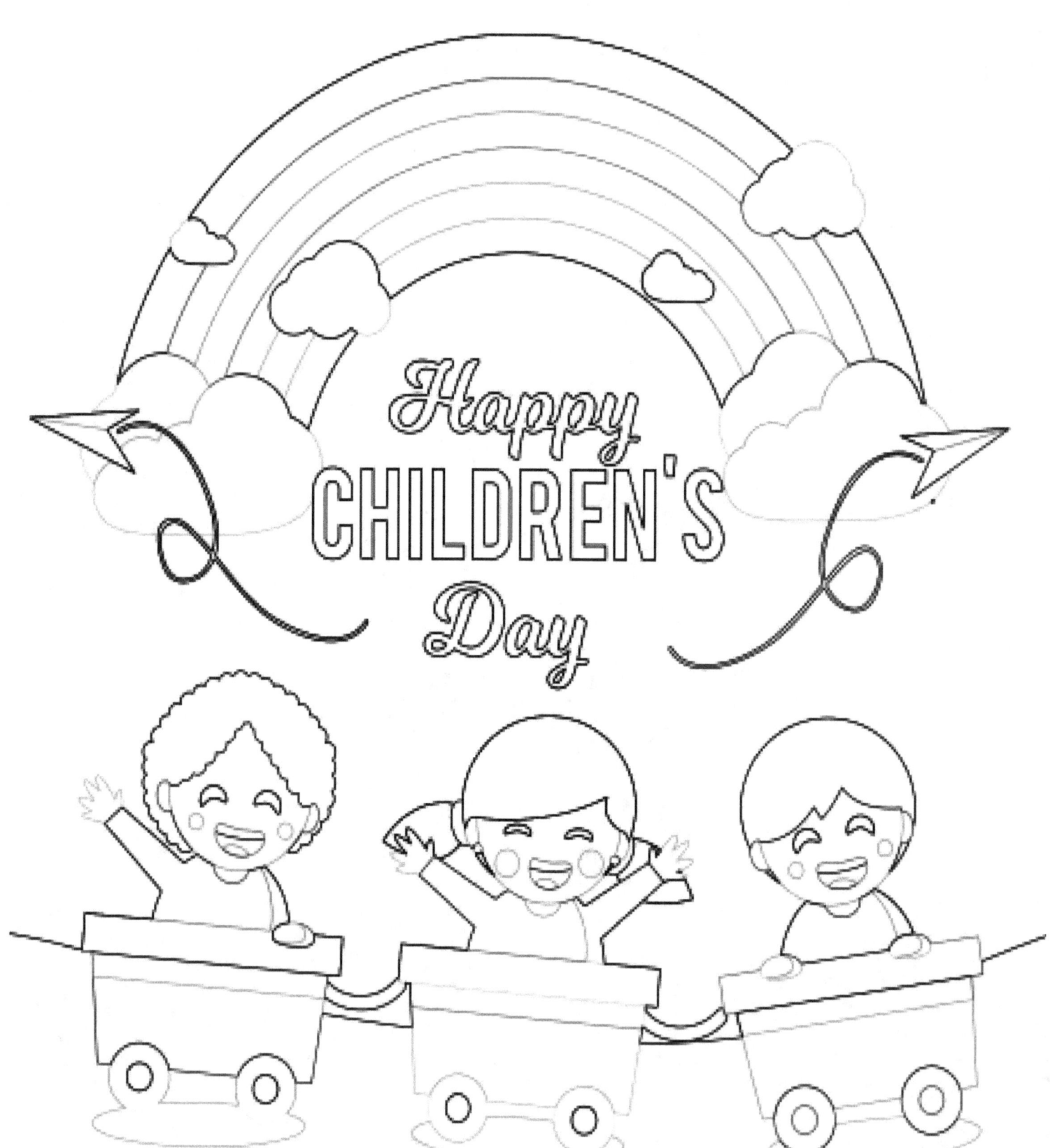

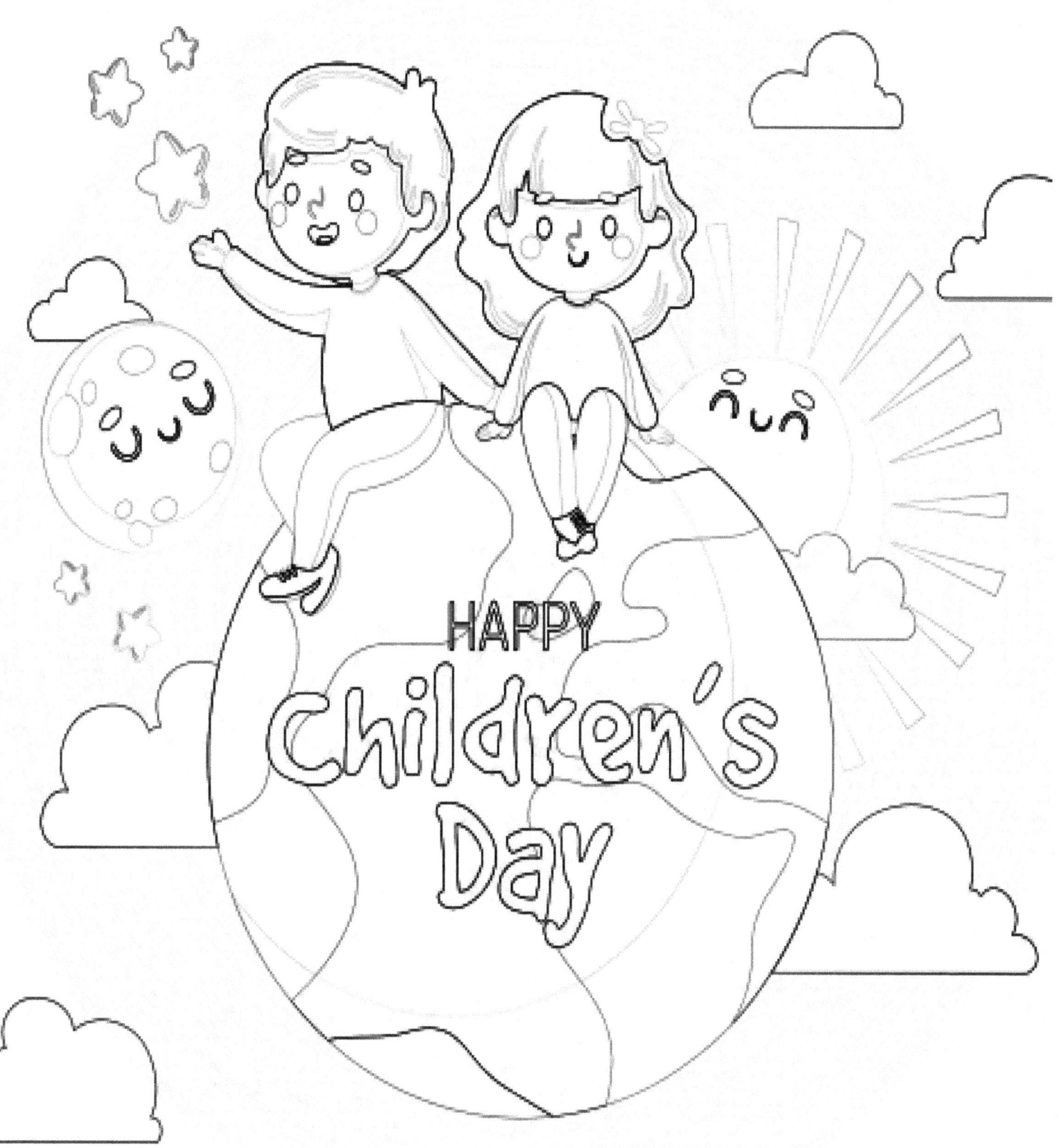

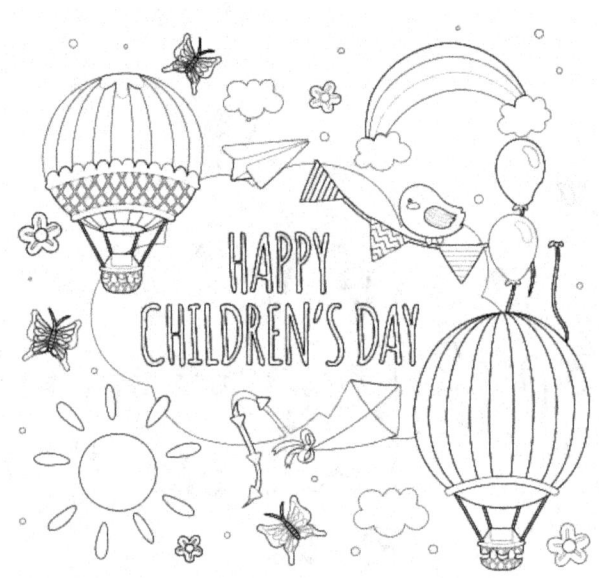

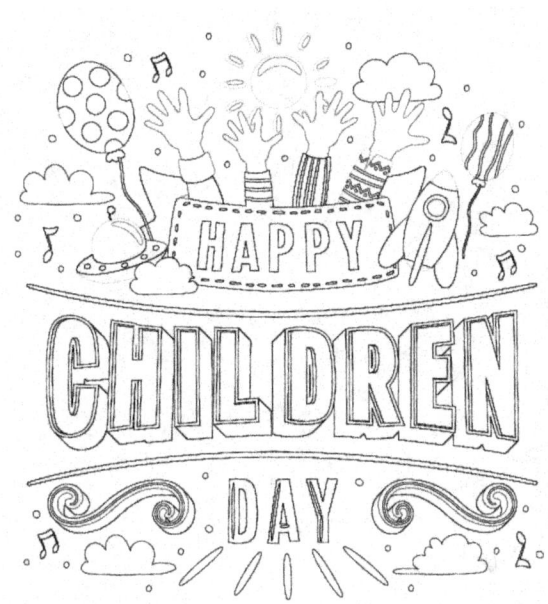

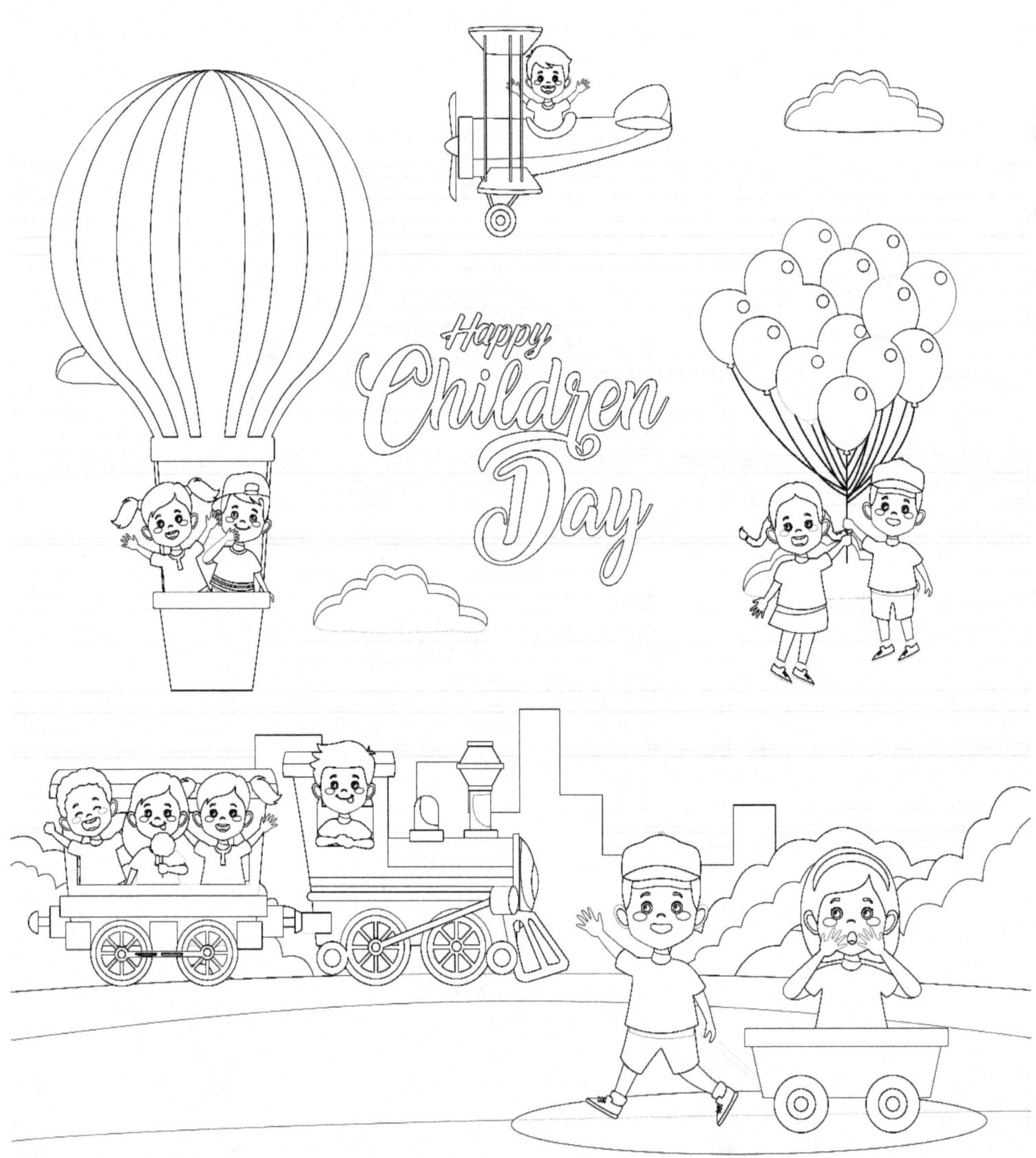

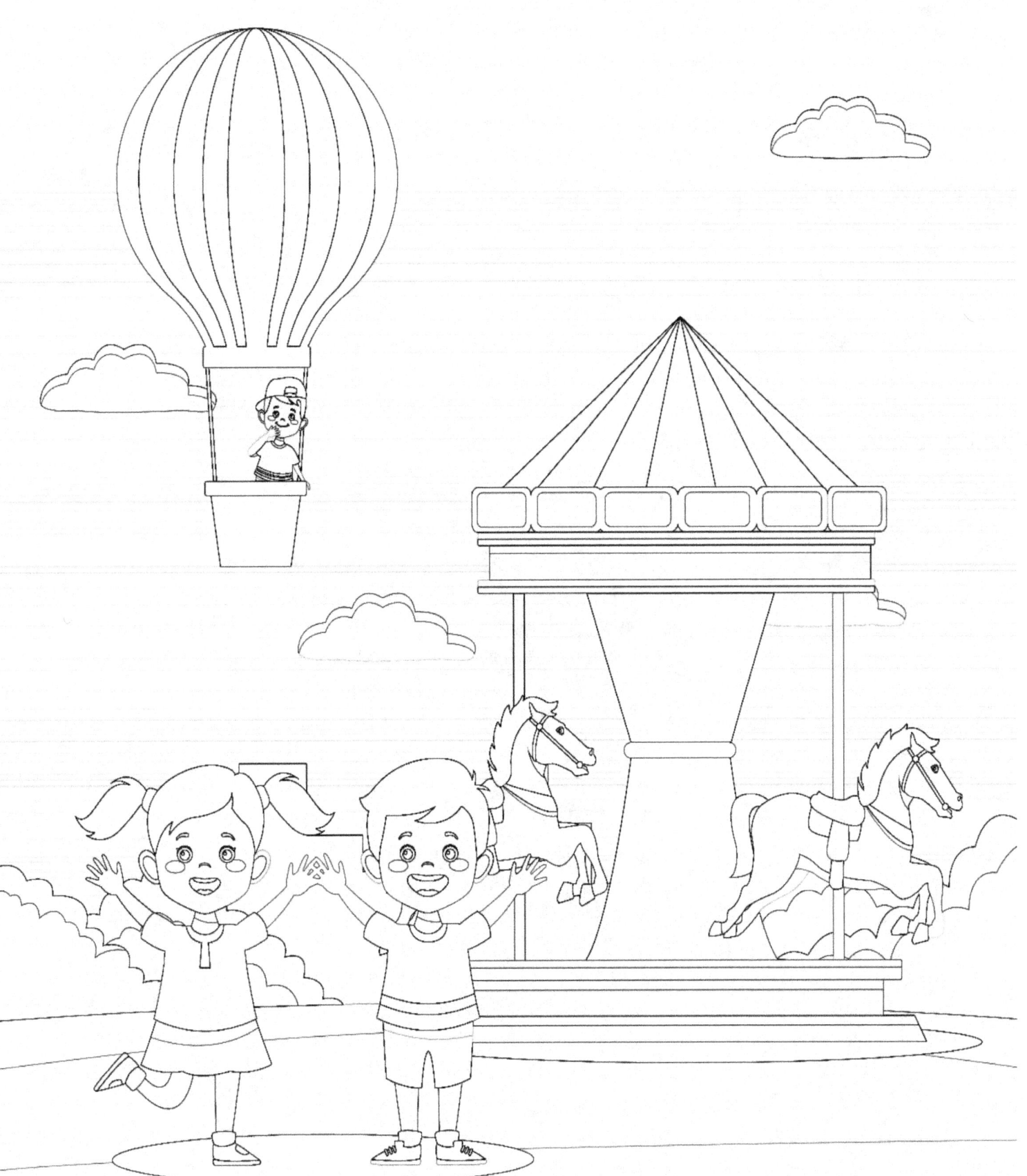

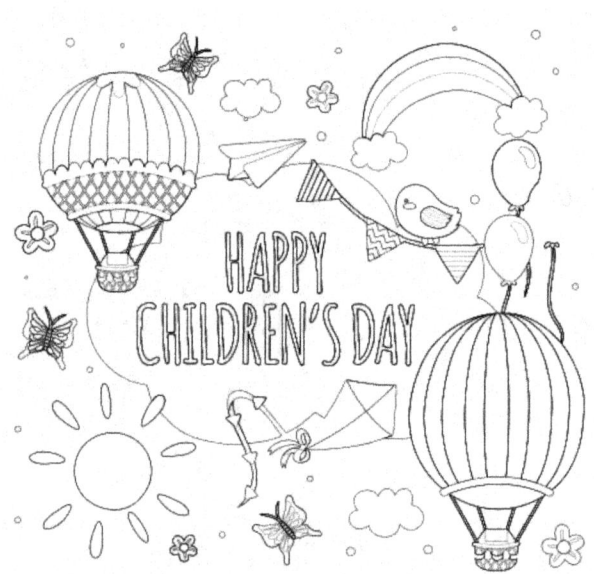

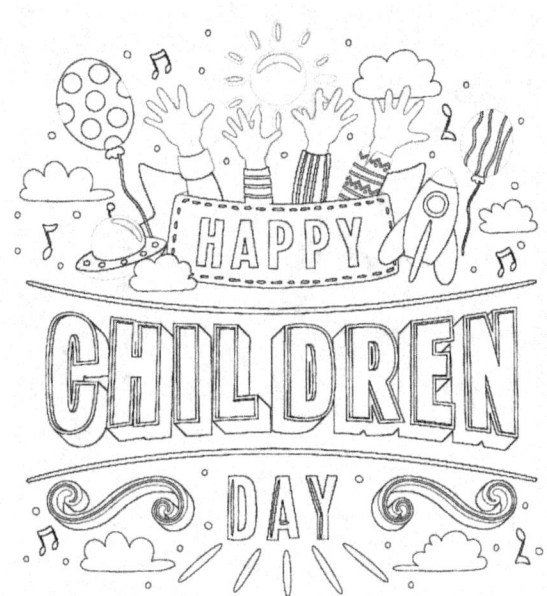

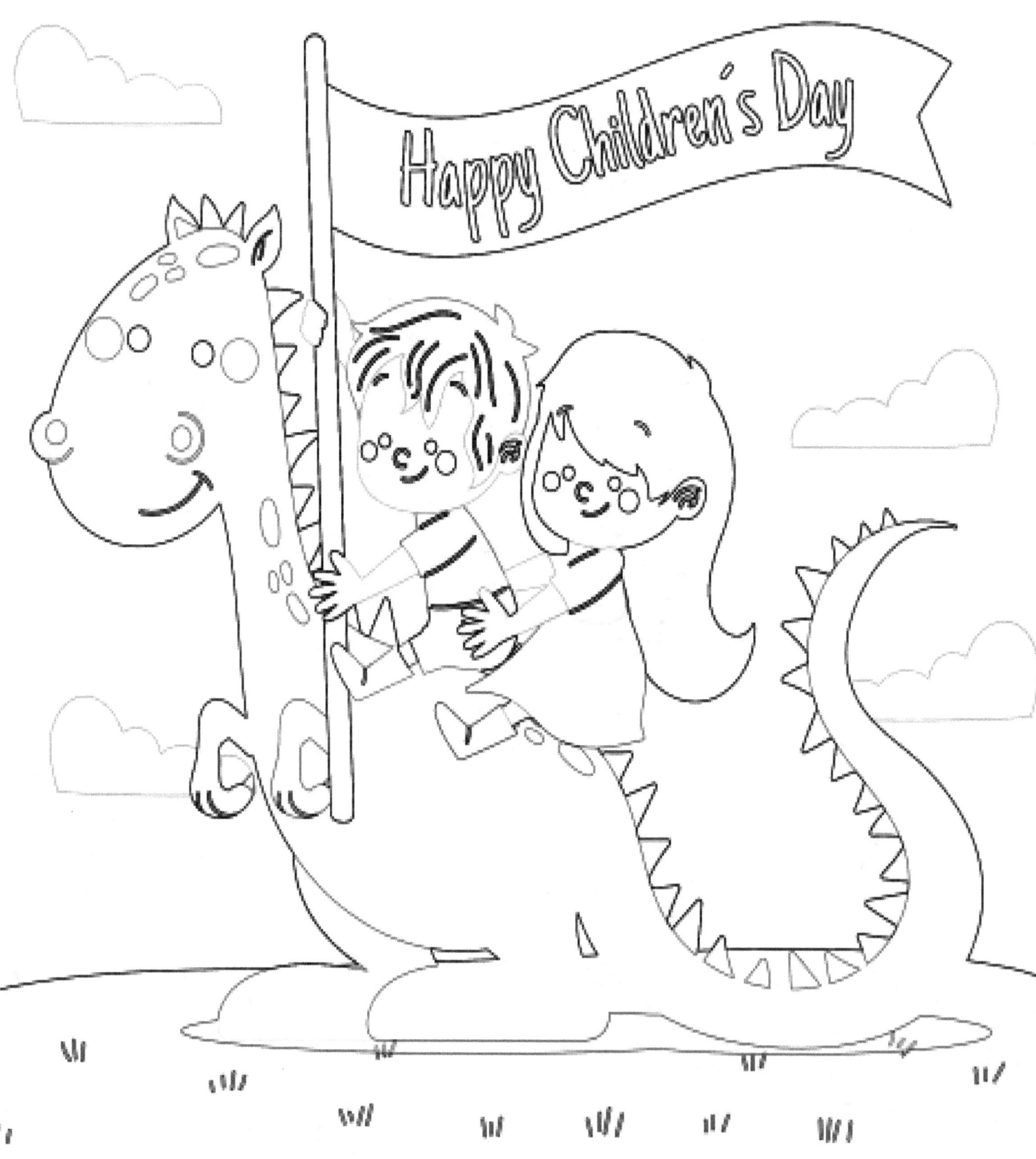

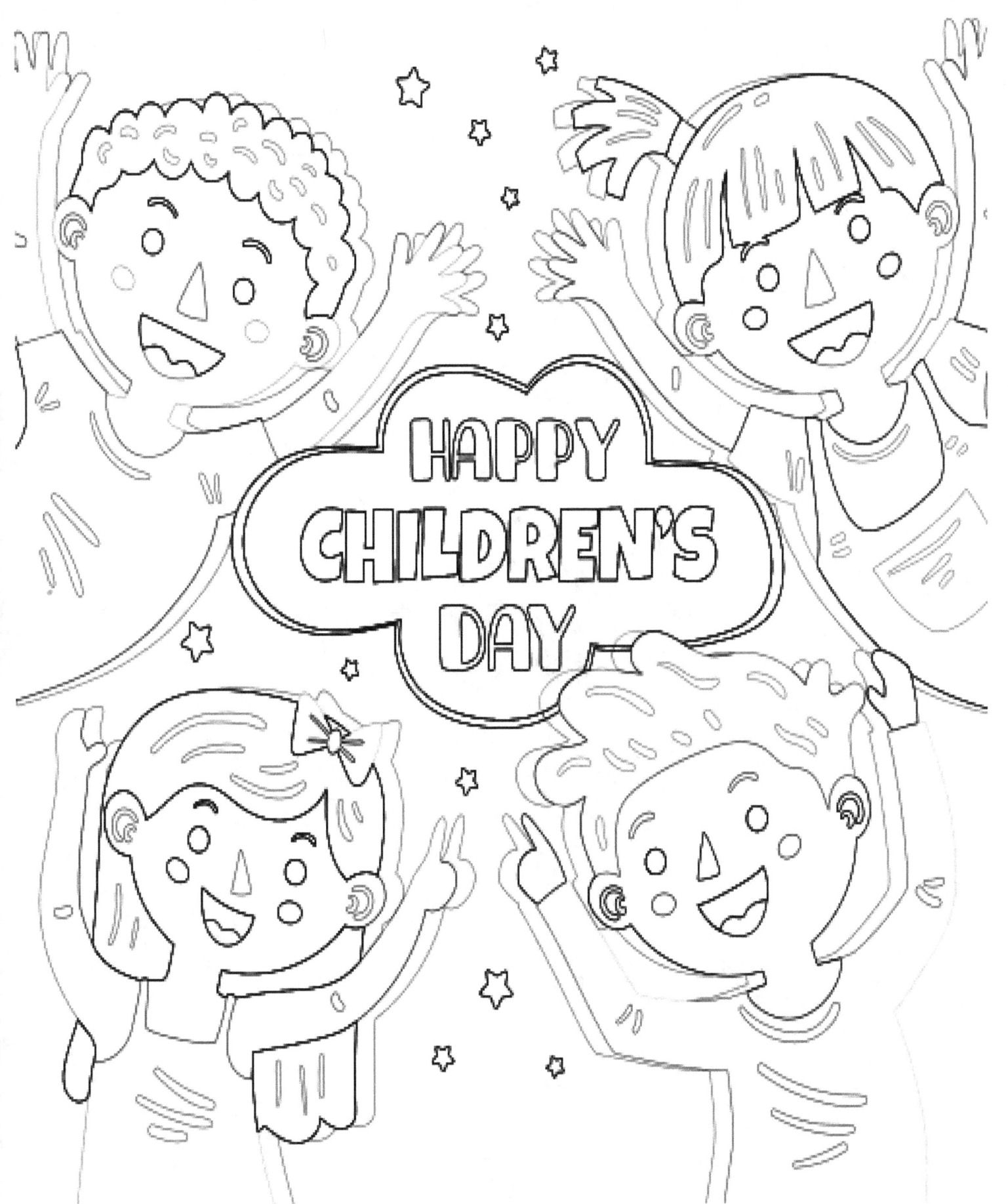

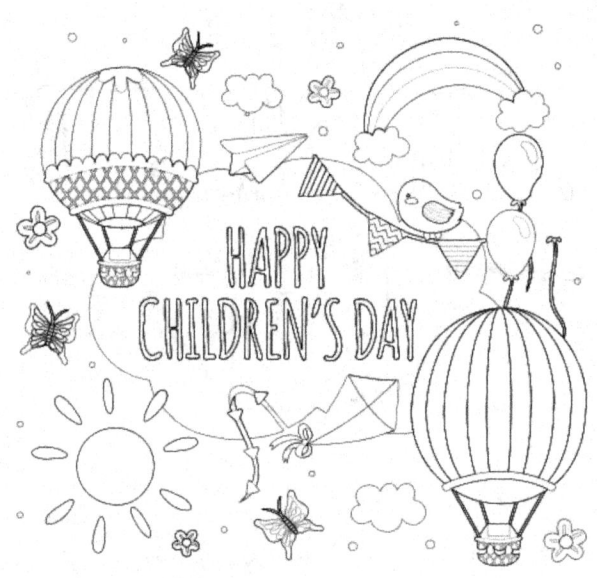

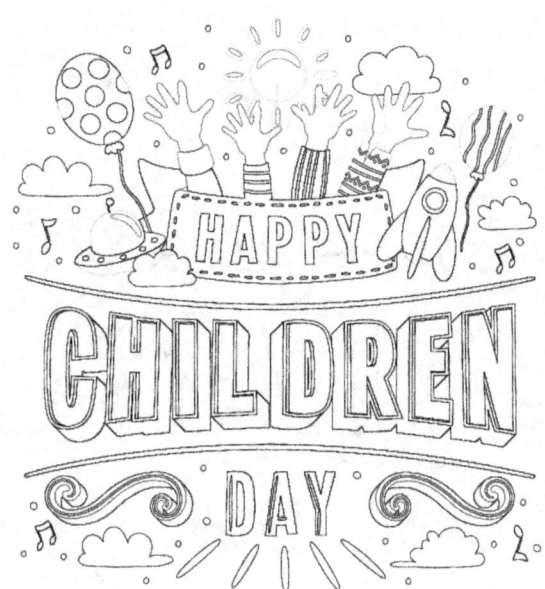

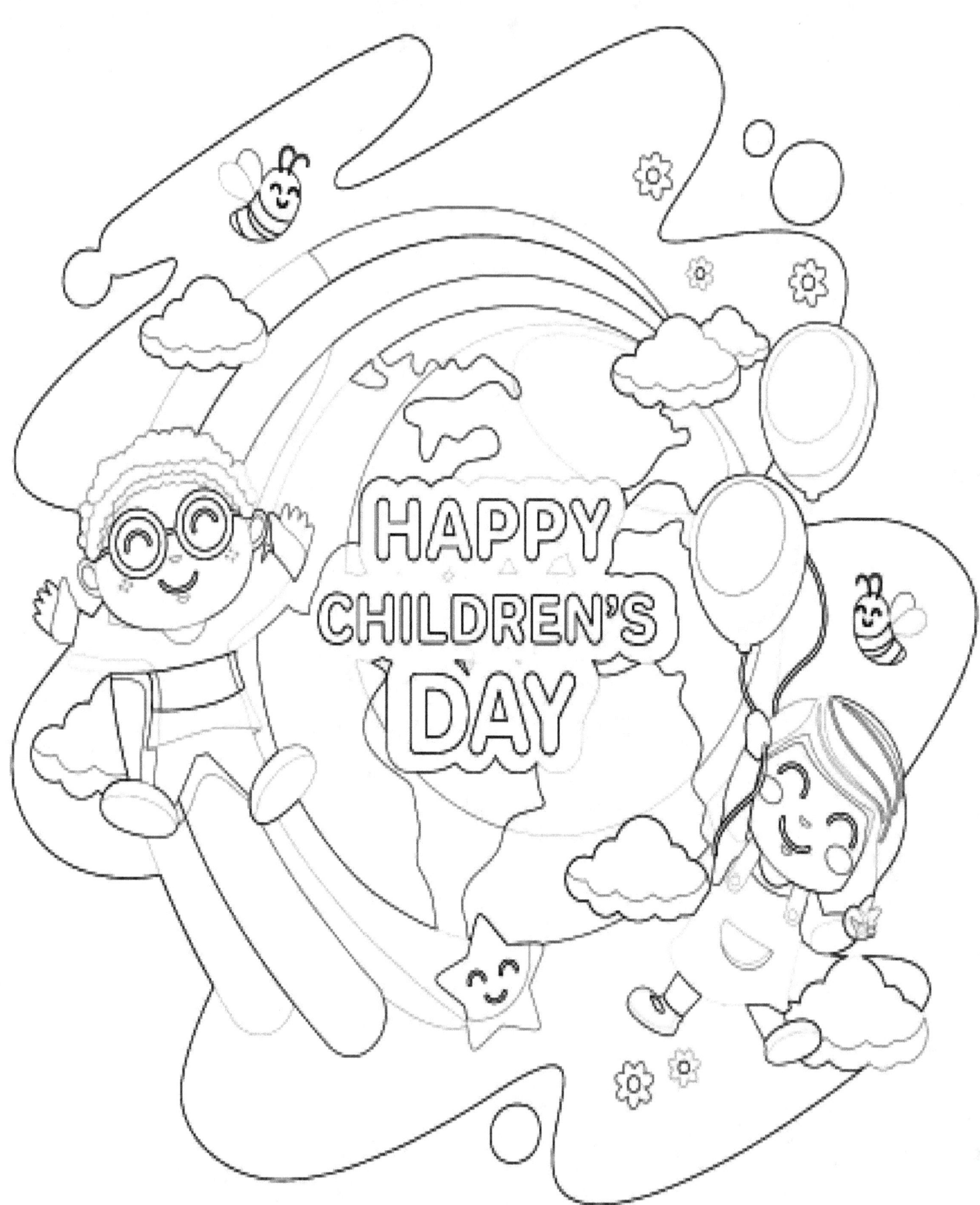

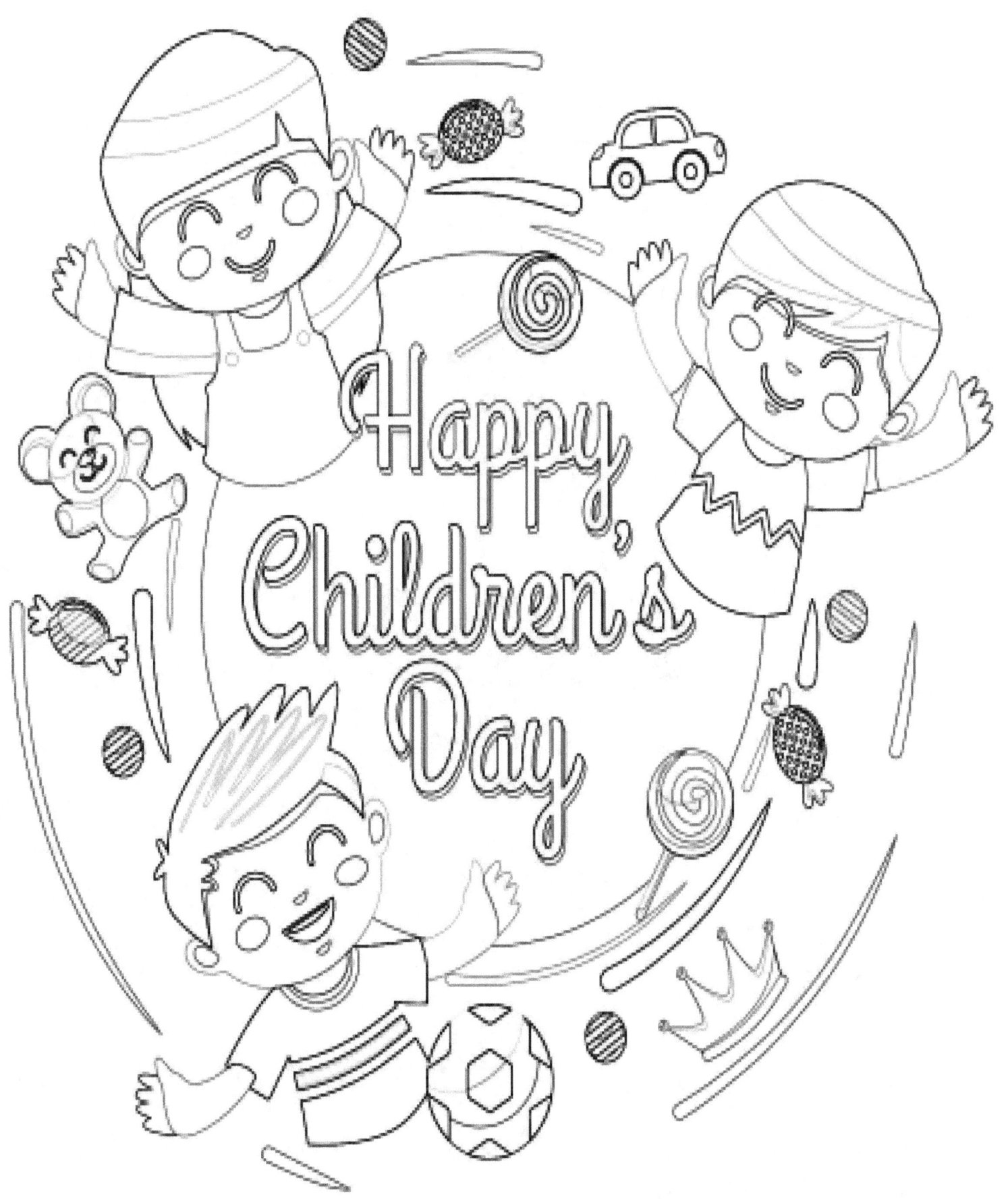

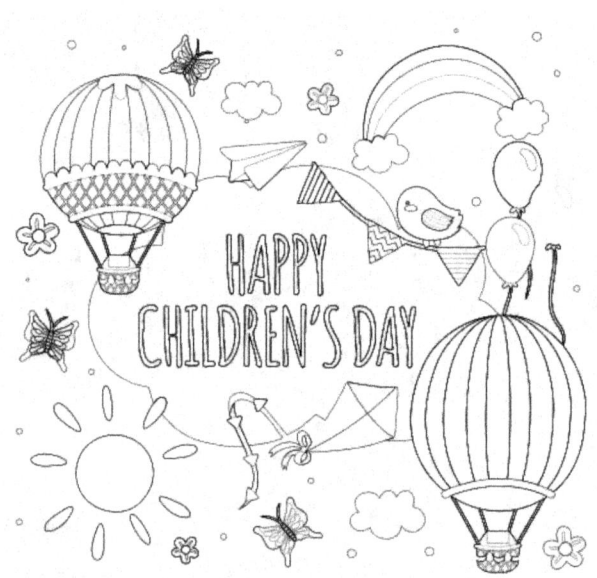

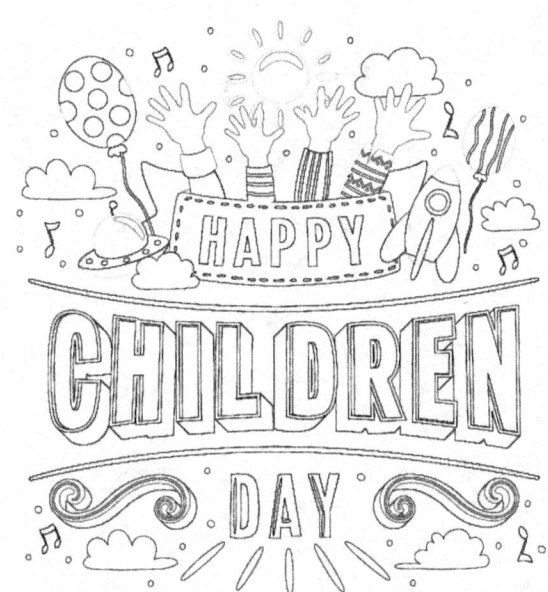

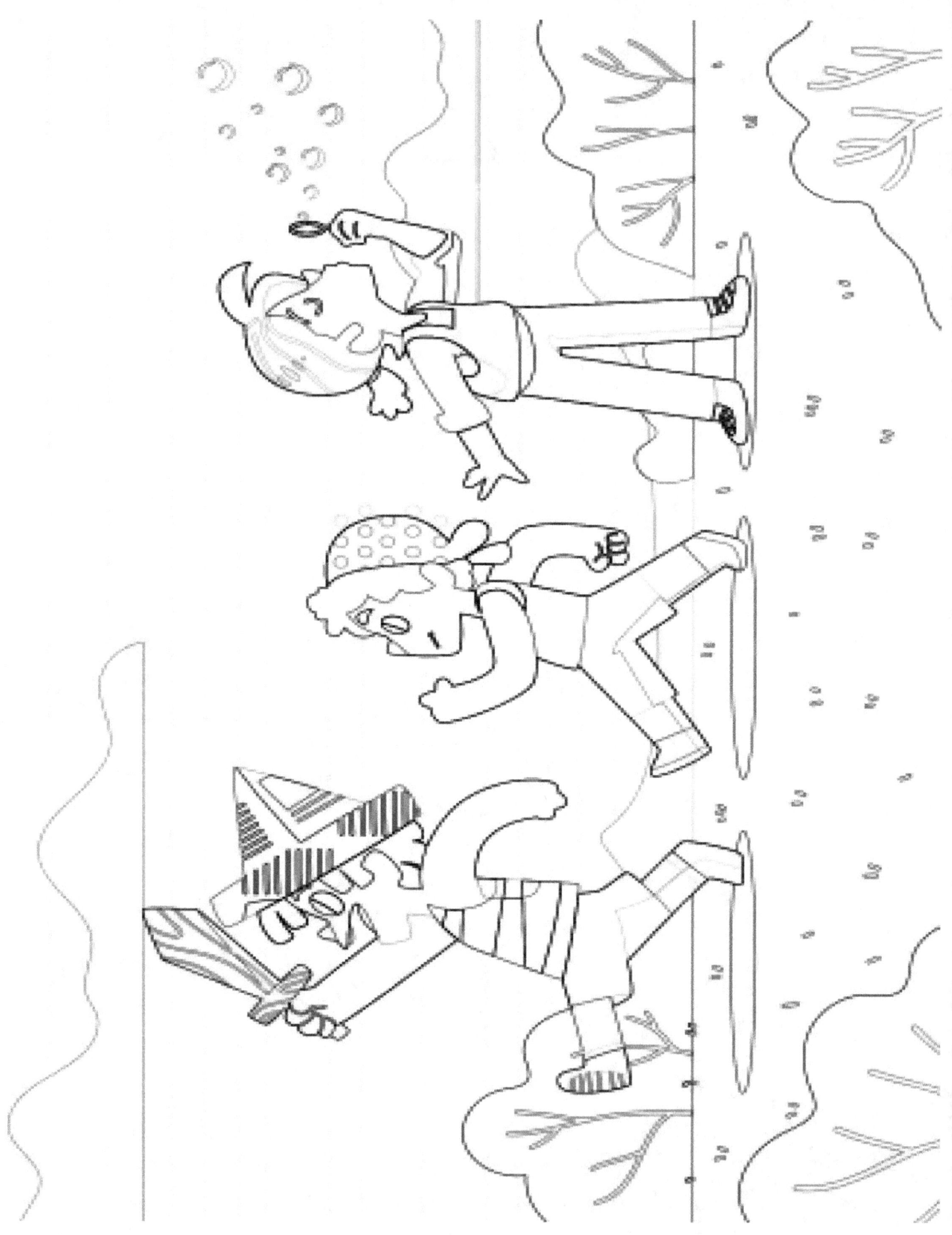

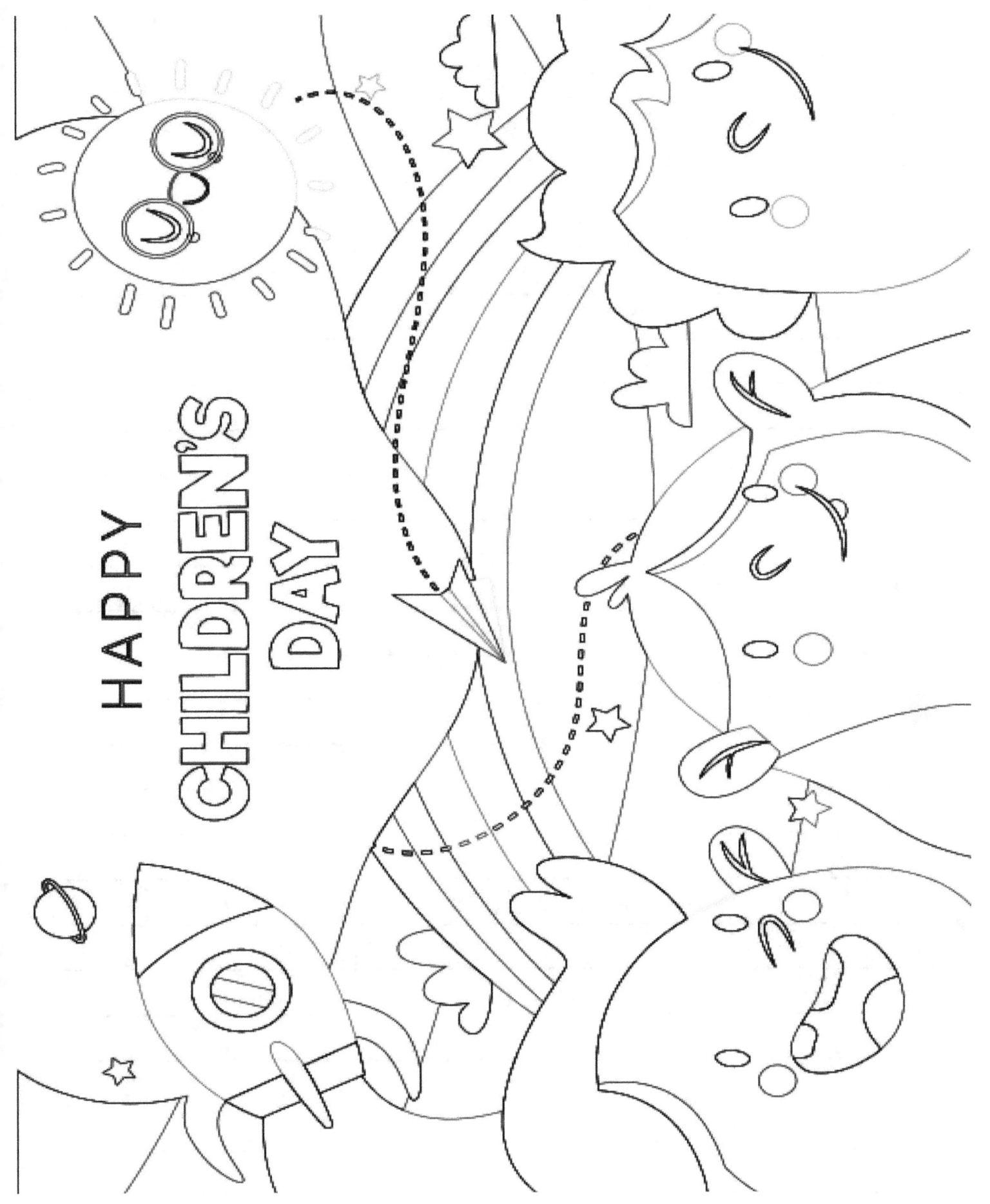

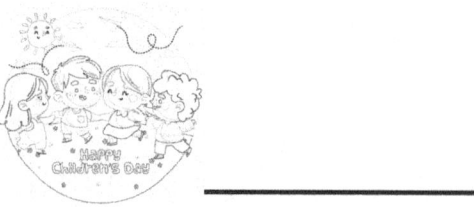

www.ingramcontent.com/pod-product-compliance
Lightning Source LLC
Chambersburg PA
CBHW081656220526
45466CB00009B/2775